Running

Across
Countries

Russell Secker

Running Across Countries

Copyright © 2009 by Russell Secker

ISBN   1448668123
EAN-13   9781448668120

CONTENTS

WARM UP 1

I DON'T LIKE MONDAYS 2
IN THE BEGINNING 7
THE ULTRA STAGE RACE FORMAT 9

RACES 15

EARLY DAYS 16
TAHOE TRIPLE – 2003 21
TRANSE GAULE – 2005 24
DEUTSCHLANDLAUF – 2007 56
LAKE TAHOE ULTRA – 2008 68
TRANS EUROPE FOOTRACE – 2009 73
   ITALY *77*
   AUSTRIA *88*
   GERMANY *90*
   SWEDEN *103*
   FINLAND *117*
   NORWAY *118*

COOL DOWN 127

A DAY IN THE LIFE 128
INTERESTING CHARACTERS 136
NERDY DATA 143

WHY? AND HOW? 145

THE BIG QUESTION 146
GETTING IT DONE 152
NUTRITION 159
SHOES 164
INJURY AND ILLNESS 165
SOME ULTRA APHORISMS 171

BIBLIOGRAPHY 175

THANKS 176

WARM UP

I DON'T LIKE MONDAYS

"People of mediocre ability sometimes achieve outstanding success because they don't know when to quit."
- George Allen, American football coach

It was a Monday in September. I had run 325 miles in the last seven days, more miles in a week than I had ever run before. Now almost halfway across Germany – between the Baltic Sea and the Swiss Alps – I was having the worst running day of my life. My feet were painful and swollen, and every step was agony. My quads were screaming at me to stop and angrily refusing to cooperate with my plan to run a 50-mile stage that day. The old Boomtown Rats song "I don't like Mondays..." was going around and around in my head. I knew I couldn't continue any longer. I was going to have to abandon the 2007 Deutschlandlauf[1] stage race with a big, fat DNF (did not finish) next to my name.

From the opposite side of the road, our Hungarian race photographer Tibor emerged with a big smile on his face, brandishing his camera and looking for a shot of me running. I waved him off, grimly gesturing with a hand across my throat that I was done, finished, *kaput*. He shrugged and walked away to look for a happier subject. Under stress like this, people often fixate irrationally; at this moment, what was upsetting me most was having to abandon my plan to get a post-race tattoo to commemorate my successful Deutschlandlauf finish. Now all that was gone.

---

[1]"Germany Run" in English.

I was 30 miles into a brutally hilly 50-mile stage. I saw my Texan running friend, Diana, who was crewing for me, running towards me. She looked desperately concerned, wearing a "what on earth can I do to keep this guy from quitting?" face. But I knew that there was nothing, absolutely nothing, she could do to keep me in the race. I was toast.

In silence, we hobbled over to the aid station at the side of the road. Di was joined by the race medic, Jan Straub, and my French friend Jean-Benoît, or J-B for short. The aid station was being manned by a local running club, and the kind volunteers looked concerned and compassionate as this piece of human wreckage arrived and slumped disconsolately into one of their canvas chairs. I shook my head and patiently explained to Jan and J-B what I had already told Di and Tibor – that, whatever they said or did, I was not going to be continuing. No ifs, ands, or buts.

They didn't appear to take my position seriously. J-B started pouring cold water on my quads and applying massage to them. Jan grabbed a cup of Coke and made me drink it, and then another, and another. Di looked on while J-B and Jan worked their magic, both pleading, admonishing and cajoling me not to quit. I just sat – silent, dejected and shell-shocked – but relieved that the torture was over.

But then something strange started to stir in my brain. Was it the sugar or the cold water or the massage? I'll never know... but I calculated that if I could cover just five more miles, I would make it to the exact halfway point in the race. "Much better to return home saying I'd made it halfway," I remember thinking. I grabbed the arms of the canvas chair, and slowly, very slowly (and very wobbly) rose to my feet. "OK, let's go," I said. The volunteers cheered, Di was incredulous and J-B pointed me down the road before I had time to change my mind. I felt the sugar kick in and knew I could reach the halfway point, even if I couldn't finish the stage. J-B and Di drove ahead in their support vehicle but never went more than a couple of hundred yards ahead of me down the road. They were staying close by, as I must've looked like I was about to keel over at any minute, and they wanted to be able to recover my soon-to-be recumbent body from the curb.

An hour or so later I'd made it to the race's midpoint. There was some consolation there and I felt slightly redeemed, but it was already very late in the day. I knew I had no chance of making the official 13 hour time cutoff. But somehow being forced to stop because I'd missed the cutoff seemed so much better than just deciding to quit. In fact, I began to relish the thought. "No more pain tomorrow," I mused. "I can return home with the knowledge that I'm not a quitter, just injured and therefore too slow to make the cutoff and stay in the race."

At about 8 p.m. that night, I made it to the finish line where my fellow competitors were sitting around a blazing campfire having a relaxing, convivial evening. They gave me the customary and rather patronizing "last finisher" cheer. I staggered into the gym and over to my mattress and sleeping bag. Di had saved me a meal from dinnertime (now three hours cold) which I dutifully ate in silence. I headed towards the shower, running into the race director, Ingo Schulze, on the way. I apologized profusely for my failure to make the cutoff and told him I realized that I was out of the race. "No, you run again tomorrow!" he cheerily told me, slapping me hard in the midsection with his race folder. My heart sank - my parole had been officially denied. I went to bed to try and sleep off the pain but silently vowed that I would not – in fact, absolutely could not – punish my feet and legs for one more day.

The next morning dawned cold and rainy. I opened my bleary eyes and saw that Di was preparing for another day of crewing. "Don't worry, I'm not running today," I told her firmly. "Oh, yes, you are," she replied, with even more conviction.

And you know what? She was right. I was back on the start line at 6 a.m. as usual. A few hours later the rain abated and we crossed the now invisible border between East and West Germany. I had come back from the dead. My feet and legs were still miserably painful but I was starting to realize that quitting is sometimes harder than continuing.

"Pain is temporary. It may last a minute, or an hour, or a day, or a year, but eventually it will subside and something else will take its place. If I quit, however, it lasts forever."
- Lance Armstrong, winner of seven Tour de France cycle races

IN THE BEGINNING

**Books can be dangerous. The best ones should be
labeled "This could change your life."**
- Helen Exley, author

There is a fine book written by Barry Lewis about
the Trans America Footrace 1992. I bought it in the
mid-'nineties and have read it from cover to cover
many times. It's a fascinating and well-written tale
of the race itself, the interpersonal dynamics
between the characters who ran in it, and the almost
insurmountable logistical difficulties of trying to put
on a stage race across a continent. The 1992 Trans
Americans were portrayed as a group of tough,
experienced, grizzled runners, who could battle
heat, cold, fatigue, injuries and hunger for days on
end. They ran huge mileages each and every day
without adequate food, water and shelter. Their
minds and bodies could withstand the physical and
emotional setbacks of the journey, and they could
for the most part accept their fate with a wry smile
and grim acceptance.

I was enormously inspired by this book and by the
eclectic yet generally humble folks who had made
their way across the US that hot summer. In one
remote corner of my mind, I thought that taking part
in a race like this would be the most fantastic
adventure. But never in my wildest dreams a
decade ago did I believe I would ever have the
chance of becoming a transcontinental runner. I was
convinced that I lacked the basic ability to run so far
and to punish my body and mind for so long. I also
never guessed that I would one day get to know two
of those thirteen Trans America finishers well –
Helmut Schieke and Stefan Schlett. Familiarity has

- 7 -

only served to increase my respect and admiration for these fine gentlemen.

But in the last five years, I can look back and know that I have done what I never thought possible. I have run across seven countries – one of them (Germany) twice. In the process of doing so, I have become a transcontinental runner too and have completed more than one hundred ultramarathons (races longer than 26.2 mile marathons). I've covered thousands of miles in training... and thousands more in races.

With all that said, know that I'm not a gifted athlete or a special person. I don't win races, although I might occasionally get lucky and pick up an age group trophy in a local 5K event. Unlike some runners, I have never been obsessive-compulsive about tracking and logging every workout, every mile and every race; neither do I have a clear record of my fastest times at every distance from the mile to the marathon. As I said, I'm not a gifted runner - for me, running is the gift itself. I am both fortunate and privileged.

For most people, the idea of running across a country – let alone a continent – represents an implausible feat of endurance. How is it possible to run for more than forty miles a day for weeks on end? And why would anyone ever want to do it? I'll try to answer those questions later in this book. But first let me describe to you the format of these ultra stage races, and then tell you about my personal experiences of running across countries as part of them.

THE ULTRA STAGE RACE FORMAT

"Do a little more each day than you think you possibly can."
- Lowell Thomas, American writer, broadcaster and traveler

Ultramarathons, or "ultras" for short, are footraces of more than 26.2 miles (or 42.2 kilometers), the standard distance for a marathon[2]. There are many ultras held regularly all over the world, ranging in distance from 50K to 100 miles or more. Perhaps the most publicized ultra is the Badwater 135, which covers that number of miles from Death Valley to Mount Whitney in insane 130 degree summer heat. There are also races based on time rather than distance, where competitors have 12, 24, 48 hours or six days to cover as much ground as possible around a looped course. These races are great feats of endurance, which require much more extensive training and racing effort than marathons or shorter distance events.

The variant of ultra running I enjoy taking part in most is ultra stage racing. This requires competitors to run more than a marathon every day for a fixed number of days, or stages. Runners typically start together each morning – and run a route laid out in what's called a "road book" and marked along the way with arrows and other visual clues – to a predetermined finish line. Winners are determined simply by total cumulative time.

---

[2] Many non-runners think that any "longer" distance running race is called a marathon, but not so.

There are a number of well organized events over shorter distances like 5, 6 or 7 days each year or for the more intrepid races lasting nearly three weeks across France and Germany. Over the last century, there have been eleven official Transcontinental stage races, in addition to a number of very heroic solo efforts. Roughly 200 runners have completed Transcontinental races (some of the 215 finishers have made more than one crossing), with a success rate of just over 40%:

1928 Bunion Derby
– Los Angeles to New York City (199 starters, 55 finishers)
1929 Bunion Derby
– New York City to Los Angeles (80 starters, 31 finishers)
1992 Trans America Footrace
– Los Angeles to New York City (28 starters, 13 finishers)
1993 Trans America Footrace
– Los Angeles to New York City (13 starters, 6 finishers)
1994 Trans America Footrace
– Los Angeles to New York City (14 starters, 5 finishers)
1995 Trans America Footrace
– Los Angeles to New York City (14 starters, 10 finishers)
2001 Trans Australia
– Perth to Canberra (24 starters, 14 finishers)
2002 Run Across America
– Los Angeles to New York City (11 starters, 8 finishers)
2003 Trans Europe Footrace
– Lisbon to Moscow (44 starters, 22 finishers)
2004 Run Across America
– Los Angeles to New York City (10 starters, 6 finishers)
2009 Trans Europe Footrace
– Bari to North Cape (67 starters, 45 finishers)

TOTALS – 504 starters, 215 finishers

Transcontinental racing across the US – once called "pedestrianism" – enjoyed brief popularity back in the depression era 'twenties, when runners from all backgrounds vied for large prize purses in C. C. Pyle's so-called "Bunion Derbies". In the 'nineties, thanks in large part to the support of the magazine Runner's World, these races resumed again – absent the large purses – at the backend of the "jogging boom." Trans Europe, Trans Australia and several more Trans America races all took place in the early part of this decade.

Stage races are remarkably simple for participants. For the most part, all runners are required to do is run, eat and sleep. A few minutes are needed each day to pack and unpack luggage and to pay attention to personal hygiene and injuries. But that's about all; the very best organized stage races don't ask any more of their participants than that. Day after day of running long distances is very hard physically and just as challenging mentally. Stages often become very formulaic and monotonous, despite changes in scenery, weather and even country.

But for race organizers, stage races are a slowly-evolving logistical nightmare. Route planning is the most crucial pre-race challenge – steering clear of large towns wherever possible and trying to keep runners on the safest roads between villages or towns willing and able to accommodate the weary travelers. Providing substantial amounts of fresh food and liquids along the way is a constant battle, especially in more remote areas. Serious things can go wrong every hour of the way – vehicle accidents, health issues or run-ins with local police, for example – and over many days this is extremely stressful for the race director. Minor problems take a toll too – like cold showers, cramped accommodations, road construction or runners missing direction signs and getting lost. It takes nerves of steel, a great support team and lots of planning to pull off a big stage race successfully.

Ultra stage races typically cost competitors at least $100 per day, for food, basic accommodation on gym floors and daily race fees. In addition, money is needed for travel to and from the race, extra food while training and racing, medicines and supplements, clothing and shoes, and to cover any loss of earnings while away from home. Bringing along a crew and support vehicle can easily add another $200 a day in cost. So a "country" race is likely to end up costing each competitor more than $3,000; a transcontinental race will work out at more than $15,000. How much prize money is usually at stake? Not a red cent.

So the financial return is negative; a plaque, certificate and T-shirt are usually the only tangible reminders of the event. Priceless, though, are the experiences, the memories and the friendships formed while on the road.

Describing these races to people isn't easy. They are so beyond most people's experience that I look for something to help them relate to the concept. The closest I can usually come up with is the Tour de France, which now receives a decent amount of TV airtime and media coverage in the US thanks to the superlative efforts of my fellow Austin resident, Lance Armstrong.

I first point out the obvious differences: we don't use bikes or get busted for using performance enhancing drugs. Unlike the Tour, there are absolutely no rest days, nor do we have support teams providing everything from massage to laundry services. There are almost no crowds nor any significant media coverage along the way, and I've never yet glimpsed a girl in a yellow dress at the finish line. Our experiences probably more closely resemble the Tour de France when it was first staged in the early nineteen hundreds. Oh, and women are actually allowed to compete, they're not just there to smooch and hand out stuffed animals at the finish of each stage.

But there are a number of similarities to the modern Tour too. Some great athletes take part, each of whom have prepared for many years to take on physical and mental challenges just as immense as the Tour's. The races last for weeks, and participants will suffer through all kinds of weather and terrain. "Road rash" is uncommon but injuries are constantly in the forefront of each runner's mind. Diet and rest are crucial and can make or break an individual's performance. And lastly, these races require prolonged absences from home, loved ones and creature comforts. The psychological strain gets more and more challenging as the race goes on, especially for athletes who are battling fatigue, injuries and illness.

RACES

EARLY DAYS

"What kind of crazy nut would spend two or three hours a day just running?"
- Steve Prefontaine in Junior High School, when he saw the High School Cross country team training

I ran my first marathon in the late '70s, and I blush to think about it. I was clueless and had absolutely no idea what I was doing. The route passed along rough country paths between several old hill forts in the south of England. The race was what would now be called a trail race, although I'm not sure that the term had been invented then. Certainly those nice, well cushioned and toe-protecting trail running shoes hadn't been. I can't remember why I signed up for this race or where I'd heard about it, but I suppose it had seemed like a good idea at the time.

What I do remember was taking an embarrassingly long time – about five hours – to finish. Embarrassing…not because of my overall time but because I was utterly clueless in my execution. I ran the first five miles insanely fast in about 30 minutes and then just died terribly, as those with more sense and experience glided past me while I slowed to a shuffle. As the expression goes these days, "the wheels had come off." Limping home hours after the winners was a chastening first marathon experience.

In the early 1980s, I moved to the US and started to train and race more sensibly and consistently for 5K and 10K distances. I decided to take another shot at the 26.2 mile distance; this time, I chose Cancun, Mexico, traveling with my then girlfriend (now my wife of 23 years), Claire. Although we had a great vacation, the marathon proved to be Disaster #2. My choice of destination had been guided by the quality of Cancun's sand, which the brochures told us had the consistency of talcum powder. The sand lived up to its fine billing, but the marathon did not. The race itself was held on Mexican Independence Day. To avoid sweltering September daytime temperatures, things got underway at midnight; even with the late start, the night-time's wicked humidity made the going very tough. I again made the rookie mistake of running the first half of the race way too fast, and so a sorry and very sick me took 3 hours 40 minutes to get finished.

As soon as I crossed the finish line, I became wretchedly ill. My stomach was turning cartwheels, and once we got back to our hotel, I developed a fierce earache. In my delirium, I staggered to the bathroom to look for some relief and accidentally substituted a squirt of shampoo for eardrops. My unconventional, lathery treatment did not work. Flying home two days later was agony as the airplane's cabin pressure increased and reduced, and only a visit to the emergency room and a close encounter with an irrigation syringe helped to alleviate the pain.

I wasn't put off by these early experiences; rather, they challenged me to train harder and race smarter, in order to realize my limited potential. I ran a number of East Coast marathons, and my times slowly started to improve with experience. One of my most vivid memories from this time was one Hallowe'en when I ran the New York City marathon. I decided to enter into the spirit of the occasion by wearing my daughter's costume, an oversized orange pumpkin shirt. Almost everyone in the estimated crowd of five million people that year yelled "Pumpkin Man" at me. It is unusual to be ridiculed by so many people in one day. I spent most of the race trying to overtake a speedy fellow dressed as Gumby, who was wearing a foam costume, green paint and sporting a rather fine Pokey the Mule around his midsection. I started to feel strange and disoriented as I crossed the finish line, became delirious and unable to move, and for the first time in my running life, ended up in the emergency tent with hypothermia[3].

In 1995, I turned 40 and entered the Marine Corps Marathon in Washington, DC. The race received an unusual amount of media coverage as that was the year in which talk-show host Oprah Winfrey decided to run. I had attempted several times to qualify for the Boston Marathon, the world's most prestigious footrace outside of the Olympics and the World Championships. To do that I needed to run a marathon time of 3 hours 20 minutes or less, but I had always missed my goal by five or ten minutes. The Marine Corps was to be my "last chance" at making it to Boston (at least until I got older, and the qualifying time would get easier).

The day got off to a very shaky start. The weather was miserably rainy and cold, and my friend Mike and I were nearly arrested by an angry DC

---

[3] Normal core body temperature in humans is self-regulated between 36.6–37.0 °C (97.9–98.6 °F). Hypothermia is a reduction in that temperature when exposed to cold. Symptoms start with shivering, fatigue and numb hands but will progress through mental confusion and eventually to death if the core temperature starts to fall below 32 °C (90 °F).

cop for peeing in public before the start. During the race, it became so foggy that at one point we nearly ran into the side of the Pentagon. (No kidding! The course route ran right through the Pentagon grounds; those were certainly kinder, gentler, pre-Homeland Security days.) Despite filthy weather, I ran a well-paced race for a change, and with a mad sprint to the finish line stopped the clock at 3 hours 19:49. I was ecstatic to have qualified for the 100th running of the Boston Marathon by just 11 seconds.

That year, Claire and I moved to Europe, where I ran a number of European marathons, including London, Dublin and Paris[4]. As my ambition and confidence grew, so did my distances; I took part in two now regrettably defunct races, the venerable London-to-Brighton 55-mile road race and the grueling 80-mile South Downs trail race, which took me an interminable 19 hours to complete.

In 2002, my career brought me back to the US, this time to Austin, Texas, a runner's paradise. Now in my late forties, I found that Austin's sunny climate enabled me to train year 'round and so, despite the onset of middle age, my overall fitness and health continued to improve. At age 48 I was even able to run the fastest marathon time of my life. But I had gotten to the point where I felt I had achieved all I was going to running marathons. I was starting to tire of training for big city events like Chicago and New York. Expensive travel and accommodation, big crowds and complicated race day logistics were really starting to bug me. I craved new, more low-

---

[4] Claire joined me to run her first two marathons in Dublin and Paris too.

key adventures.

Online research had turned up a multiday race called the Transe Gaule[5]. It looked really cool, and as a francophile, I started to dream of running from the English Channel and across rural France to the Mediterranean with a small, cosmopolitan group of runners. But I knew that I needed to test myself with a stage race first to see whether I would actually be able to run the kinds of distances involved – further than a marathon, day after day. Then I learned about the Tahoe Triple.

---

[5] A French play on words, literally meaning Gallic fright or dream.

TAHOE TRIPLE – 2003

"The greatest pleasure in life is doing the things people say we cannot do."
- Walter Bagehot

The last week of September is a great time to be a runner in Lake Tahoe. Cool nights and glorious sunny days dominate, and the pine forests give off a beautiful scent to match the scenery. Each year, runners can choose between 5K, 10K, Half Marathon, Marathon, Triple Marathon and 72-mile Ultra. In other words, something for everyone.

For the Triple, runners circumnavigate Lake Tahoe on the California-Nevada border in three daily segments, each of which is the length of a regular 26.2 mile marathon. The entire course sits between sixty-two hundred and seven thousand feet of altitude and there are plenty of hills, so it's definitely not for the faint-hearted. I entered the Tahoe Triple as a test for the Transe Gaule and as a way to qualify for it.

My preparations for the race, which had been going oh so well, were suddenly interrupted by a serious bike accident. Six weeks before the race, I was out riding with my wife when our wheels touched. The next thing I remember was being put on a backboard by a paramedic and taken to the nearest hospital. I'd wiped out and done a full "face plant" only half a mile from my home. I was in tremendous pain. My helmet, which I believe to this day saved my life, had cracked in half. It took a full week before I could lie down without major back spasms. Sneezing was crucifying. I had four days of memory loss and was off work for ten. Four weeks before the race was due to start, I took my first tentative running steps, only making it 50 feet to the end of our driveway before the pain became too much. I couldn't see how I was going to take on the challenge of three marathons back-to-back, but I persevered...and day by day, things slowly improved. Three days before the start, Claire and I nervously headed off to Nevada.

Tahoe was a revelation. It is a beautiful place, the second deepest lake in North America. The air is clean, the views spectacular and the fall climate very runner friendly. I found that I liked the stage race format a lot, and really enjoyed getting to know the other competitors. Stage racing tests both mental and physical strengths of a runner, and Tahoe was a great way to see if I had enough of both of those two things. I ended up finishing 6th overall, pacing each day well by starting conservatively and finishing strongly. Based on advice from three-time winner Sean Meissner, Claire made me stand in the very cold lake after each day's race to prevent swelling in my legs. I'm not sure if that's what did the trick, but if nothing else she seemed to enjoy my daily dose of misery.

After an extended afternoon nap, I ate fettucine alfredo and salad at a local Italian restaurant each night. Every morning I got up at 5 a.m. and ate large amounts of cereal, English muffins and bananas. This diet seemed to work for me like a charm, with no hint of "bonking" (energy depletion) late in the race or stomach issues.

Over the course of the three days, I lost several toenails due to running down the course's steep descents wearing shoes with toe boxes slightly too snug. As ultra runners know, you learn something from every race, and getting my shoe fit right was my big takeaway from Tahoe. Otherwise, I felt good about going longer and farther. I returned to Austin confident, optimistic and ready to sign up for the Transe Gaule.

TRANSE GAULE – 2005

**"France, and the whole of Europe, have a great culture
and an amazing history. Most important thing though
is that people there know how to live! In America
they've forgotten all about it. I'm afraid that the
American culture is a disaster."**
- Johnny Depp

We kicked off our first management meeting of the
year by discussing New Year's resolutions. We were
each asked to describe our personal aspirations for
2005. While others took some time to consider the
question, I blurted out without hesitation: "My goal
this year is to run across France." My statement was
met with blank looks. My colleagues – tending to be
both overweight and under-exercised – clearly
thought the idea so far out in left-field that it

sounded, well, crazy. As we went around the room, some described their more modest hopes, like "losing some weight" or "going to the gym more." I silently concluded that my resolution was more inspiring...and probably more likely.

I left Austin for Paris in August, six days before the race started. From there, I took a train to the coastal town of Roscoff, where I waited for three days for the start of the Transe Gaule. Training had generally gone well. Being a stubborn, independent guy, I had made up my own training program. Since I lived 12 miles from work (which fortunately possessed a shower and changing facilities), I improvised by running "two a day" workouts to and from the office. It was a brutally hot Texas summer. My morning 12-miler was often run in 95% humidity, and my late afternoon return trip was in 100°F (38°C) heat. My motto was the overworked Nietzsche quote, "What does not kill me, makes me stronger."

My biggest concern from the start of this adventure was injury. Years of running takes its toll on the legs and feet. I'd had knee cartilage surgery in 1999 after which my surgeon advised me never to run another marathon again. On top of that, I'd had some Achilles tendon, hamstring and lower back issues. But all things considered, this was stuff I thought I could handle. I megadosed glucosamine and cod liver oil, hoping for the best.

Almost everything else had held together well. As I headed towards the start, my only really troubling injury was somewhere deep inside my left foot: an odd, grisly lump right under the ball of the foot. For the most part, this didn't trouble me when I ran. But on longer runs, I started getting shooting pains in my second and third toes. Podiatry hadn't helped and different shoes only made the problem worse, never better.

My co-workers knew I was taking part in the Transe Gaule. I enjoyed their support but felt lots of pressure – pressure to finish, pressure to do well, pressure to keep moving through the really bad, inevitably awful times. I wanted so badly to do well, but as the race approached I started to feel more and more nervous about the daunting distances ahead of me. Forty miles a day for eighteen days sounds like a long way when you're months or years before the event. But as the start closed in, forty miles stopped being so abstract and started to sound like a very real – and a very long – challenge. At least I believed that I had prepared tolerably well. I was comfortably running 15 mile training runs at 7 mph or better and I'd been putting in a number of 100-mile training weeks, thanks to my 12 mile commutes on foot to and from work.

I kept reminding myself of two things: that I must run conservatively during the first few stages, and that the last third of each days' 40 miles would seem endless. Anyone who has run a marathon or two knows that the last six miles will always feel somewhere between bad and gut-wrenchingly miserable. That's how the last ten miles of each day in France would feel. Miserable. Nothing left. Dull, sore legs. Painful feet. I needed to expect that and be ready to deal with it - to be "in the moment" each day, enjoying the freedom, the feeling of just getting it done. Wimping out could not be an option.

With a little help, I had managed to create a blog for

my event so that folks could track my progress across France. I hoped to be able to post to it from my PDA, but I had no idea whether the technology would work in France. On my last day at work before leaving Austin, my company organized an amazing send-off for me: wine, cheese, French music and a toast. My part was to run into the auditorium and get applauded. Not too tough to handle! Even Claire and my teenage sons Rob and Tom were there. It was an exciting, emotional moment. I let everyone know that my goal was to finish, reminding folks that 40% usually have to abandon.

On the morning I left, Claire took me to the airport at 5 a.m. I knew I'd miss her lots for the next three weeks, but was glad that she decided to stay home with our sons whose new school year was about to begin. I knew she'd be a wreck with the uncertainty of this adventure.

My left foot felt very uncomfortable flying between Dallas and Boston – worryingly so. During the flight, I re-read the accounts of the previous year's race, along with the description of injuries battled by some of the competitors, which this did nothing to calm my nervousness. Thankfully the discomfort passed before I boarded the Paris leg of the journey.

My flight to Paris was uneventful, made nicer by an upgrade to business class. From Charles de Gaule airport, I took a bus to the Montparnasse district and walked a few blocks to the euphemistically named Comfort Inn where I was staying for a night. After a few hours' catch up on sleep, I took a run down the Boulevard des Invalides and over the Seine, eventually making my way to the Bois de Boulogne. I love Paris and know it well enough to get around without a map. I ran easily for two hours and everything felt good, especially the moderate temperatures after baking through the Texas heat all summer. "I'm ready," I thought.

Returning to my hotel, I spent some happy time battling with technology. My PDA didn't seem to work at all in France – no network signal. My French cell phone was functional, but its prepaid credits seemed to evaporate just getting the damned thing to work. Even more worryingly, the electric outlets wouldn't take my French power adaptors, so recharging was impossible. When I finally gave up on technology, I headed back to Gare Montparnasse to collect my train ticket to Roscoff, then later walked for another couple of hours back to the Champs-Elysée to get dinner. I hoped that spending a lot of time on my feet would prove useful.

The next day I traveled by high speed TGV (*Train Grande Vitesse*) from Paris to Roscoff and had three days to rest and acclimate before the race. TGVs are a wonderful way to travel – high speed, comfortable, low stress and environmentally friendly. During the journey, I tried to distract myself by finishing Maarten Troost's excellent book, "Sex Lives of Cannibals." As I watched the French landscape fly by in a blur, the sight was wonderful but scary. I calculated that it was over 300 miles to Roscoff, which we covered in four hours. This same distance on the Transe Gaule would take eight days to run. It seemed such a long way but oh-so-beautiful at the same time. I couldn't wait to get underway.

I spent a couple of peaceful, relaxing days in the quaint seaside town of Roscoff before the start of the race. At local shops, I managed to buy some fresh fruit and a large quantity of fruit loaf (*Cake Anglais*). This would prove to be a main staple for many uninspiring Transe Gaule breakfasts ahead, which unfortunately the race organization didn't provide that year. I ran comfortably for an hour or so to the next village, St Pol-de-Leon, to stay loose and to remind my legs of what lay ahead. The Garmin®[6] that Claire had given me as a birthday gift was working OK, but I was having problems recharging its battery. I never did get that charger to work again[7], but luckily I was able to borrow another competitor's each night.

On the day before the race, I met race director Jean-Benoît Jaouen (now known to me as J-B, pronounced Jee-Bay) for the first time. Since our first meeting, J-B has become a great friend, and has gotten me through some very tough times on the road. He was once a software guy, but now spends his life devoted to running and writing about it for magazines. Some of each year he spends in Brittany and some in Central America; the rest of his time is spent racing or race directing. His calm, thoughtful yet dynamic demeanor is perfectly suited to dealing with the day-to-day stress of directing ultra stage races.

I also met for the first time three of his fine race volunteers (*bénévoles* in French) - Jacquemine, Jacques and Philippe. Volunteers play a critical role

---

[6] This is a global positioning system (GPS) device, worn like a wristwatch, which uses orbiting satellites to determine location, distance traveled and speed.
[7] When I returned to the US, I called Garmin® to report my problem. Without any questions, they shipped me a replacement free of charge – what wonderful customer service!

in any stage race. They provide clean-up services in the morning, baggage handling, food and drinks at aid stations along the course and last but not least help with evening meals. Their selfless mission is to help tired and grumpy stage runners reach the finish line each day. It's a noble calling.

J-B took us to a reception at the *Mairie* followed by press interviews and photographs. I was starting to feel semi-famous, but I was unsure that I could live up to the early billing of extreme ultra runner. After the reception, we all drove together to the seafront vacation home of a friend of the Transe Gaule for a wonderful French lunch – a whole roast pig.

Just after we got there, Janne Kankaansyrja from Finland and Hiroko Okiyama from Japan made their first appearances. Both had run Trans Europe (Lisbon to Moscow) in 2003. Janne placed fifth overall. Hiroko had abandoned after 42 days because her leg literally snapped, forcing her to stop. I found myself in awe of these incredible athletes. During lunch, Jacques also told his fascinating story. As an accomplished runner himself, he'd cycled around the world for seven and a half years when he finally could stand his office job no longer. Now there's extreme for you! His adventures are documented in his book, *Cyclo Nomad.*

Seeing these super skinny but well-toned athletes, I was reminded of an observation that one of my great friends, Pete O'Hagan, once made: "I feel like a Kenyan when I stand next to normal people. When I'm with real runners, I feel like a sumo wrestler!" For the first time, I was getting that sumo wrestler feeling and starting to understand how hard this race was going to be.

THE RACE

The next morning, we congregated at the start line in Roscoff at about 7:30 a.m. right by the shoreline. The scene was one of confusion and disorder. J-B was trying to get everything organized by the time the Mayor of Roscoff arrived to start the race. He'd managed to procure a sound system from somewhere, which he used to introduce the competitors. We each stepped forward and took a bow. Although the race was due to begin at 8 a.m., things were still pretty disorganized half an hour after that. But eventually, a black-and-white Breton flag was lowered, and we all set off together as a group for the first 10km "prologue" to St Pol-de-Leon, where the race proper was to start.

It was interesting to observe how the group set out on Stage 1. Some were clearly "chomping at the bit" with pent-up energy to spare. The Brazilian marine Sebastiaõ Ferreira da Guia was particularly wound up and ready to start hammering down the road. Others with more multi-day experience took things easier. I found myself somewhere in between. As J-B drove his race vehicle past us during the early going, he gestured to everyone to slow down and be conservative, reminding us that a long road lay ahead. Sound advice!

By the time I made it to the finish line at Plounévézel, I had exceeded all my expectations. I finished in a ridiculously high fourth place, after Janne, Sebastiaõ and Hiroko. Early in the stage, I had moved ahead of many good runners: Trond Sjåvik from Norway; a Dutch guest runner and previous female Transe Gaule winner, Ria Buiten; Jan Ondrus, a Czech medical doctor; and Frenchman and former boxer Fabrice Rosa. Towards the end of the stage, I caught another Frenchman, Bernard Constant, who eventually placed third in the overall rankings. Bernard was sitting by the side of the road trying to deal with leg cramps, which I later discovered had affected lots of runners. I'd avoided cramps and felt pretty good at the end of the day, despite the effects of heat and distance. After training in the Texas heat, temperatures merely in the eighties seemed just fine with me.

I called Claire on my cell phone as I lounged at the finish line - still enjoying my endorphin high - thrilled to tell her that I had done well and had finished ahead of so many good runners. She was less than pleased and quickly brought me down to earth. I received an appropriate dressing down – or "bollocking" as we call it in England – for going off too hard on the first day. I'd tried to relax and take it easy but the pent-up excitement was too much to hold back; adrenalin had kicked in fiercely. Over the next few days, I would pay the price for my over-eager first day.

Our first night's dinner at the gym in Plounévézel was a wonderful buffet spread of salads, spaghetti, bread, wine and fruit. I sat next to a very nice English lady, Susan, who was spending a few days with the race as Bernard's helper. Susan lives with her husband in the south of France, and in the first few days of the race acted as English translator for J-B, a responsibility that would later fall to me.

We were all supposed to turn in at 9:30 p.m. Later in the race, folks seemed to drift off to sleep much quicker due to the cumulative fatigue, but during the early days, many couldn't relax as quickly, and the gyms were often noisy and too brightly lit until 11 p.m. or so. Before bedtime, I carried out for the first time what turned out to be my evening ritual. I laid out all my stuff for the next day: the course map and directions; clean clothes; band-aids for my nipples; Vaseline; and gel and power bars. I had worked out a system for sharing a charger with the other Garmin® owner, Jean-Hervé Duchesne, and so I made sure that both our GPS devices were fully charged. Finally, I started an uncomfortable and fitful sleep that was over way too soon at 5 a.m. the next morning.

The second stage was naturally much harder for me. I started to develop stomach problems during the middle section of the race, six miles of which was along the lovely Nantes-Brest Canal. Despite the wonderful scenery, I was really not able to enjoy it. My hamstrings were very tight and I didn't want to push the pace and risk worse problems, so I walked quite a few of the many, long hills. All of the folks I'd passed on Day 1 beat me, as well as some who hadn't, such as Laurent Bruyère and Daniel Muller, leaving me in a weary tenth place. After the race, a reporter came to the finish line and interviewed and photographed us. I was beginning to feel like a poor man's David Beckham!

J-B's race organization had started to click and was really impressive. In a word that works equally well in French or English, *impeccable*! Great course maps and road markings were provided, while wonderful volunteers – Jacquemine, Jacques, Charles and Philippe, plus a lovely couple Marcel and Marie-Louise – were all first class, upbeat, knowledgable and supportive.

A company called Bolino sponsors the Transe Gaule each year and is a maker of dehydrated "cup noodle" type products, which proved to be a wonderful thing at the end of the day's running. For the first time, I apprehensively tried *parmentier*[8] (an approximation of Shepherd's Pie), which proved strangely tasty and edible! Or perhaps I was just hungry? As the race progressed, I found I was actually able to consume Bolinos at aid stations mid-race. Before the Transe Gaule, I would never have thought this digestively possible.

Stage 3 proved to be a better one for me. Well, OK, maybe slightly 'flukey' as I again managed to finished in fourth place. Trond, the Norwegian, who'd been a fair distance ahead of me earlier in the day, got lost after missing the sign onto the final 11-mile path to the finish line in the village of Guer. I would've missed it too if a local hadn't pointed it out to me. Poor Trond ended up running quite a few extra kilometers that day.

---

[8] It turns out that Antoine-Augustin Parmentier was a vocal promoter of the potato as a food source for humans in France and throughout Europe two centuries ago. Google him - his life story is really a fascinating one.

As we headed towards Châteaubriant on Day 4, my shins started to bother me early in the day and never relented. I completed the fairly flat 42 miles in reasonable shape and finished sixth overall, behind Janne, Trond, Sebastiaõ, Jan and Bernard but ahead of Hiroko and Fabrice Rosa. Lots of folks were noticeably limping around the gym at the end of the day. The next few stages were going to be tough for many of us, including me.

Janne had won for a fourth time, and would go on to dominate every stage. I had started to befriend Bernard, as we were running at a similar pace but most of the time his thick accent prevented me from understanding much of his French. Like the previous day, he did the same thing on this stage – went flying off too fast, died in the middle of the race, and then finished like a greyhound. I was interested to see how he would manage on future days without the aid of his helper, Susan, who had to return to her home in the south of France.

After I'd made my camp in the school gym and rested for an hour, I staggered nearly a mile and back to the shops in the center of Châteaubriant. On the way, I ran into Trond and offered to buy him a cup of coffee at a roadside café. This was the first time I'd really spoken to this fine Norwegian, and I got to know and respect him more with each passing day of the race. In town, I bought lots of stuff in the supermarket – salads, salami, tea, sugar, chocolate, and bread – and ate well, saving some provisions for the next day.

For a psychological boost, I had arranged to meet up with an Australian friend Raife and his fiancée from New Zealand, Victoria. I had worked with Raife in

London for a couple of years but had never met his future life partner Vik. They were touring France on their tandem and adjusted their plans so that they could meet me *en route*. I knew I had to start the day conservatively and then hold on through the inevitable discomfort, so I could be in a fit state to enjoy their company.

Getting from Châteaubriant to St Georges-sur-Loire was by far the hardest stage yet. My shins continued to give me a lot of pain, especially at the start, and I was limping along in the *peloton*[9] for much of the day with Fabrice Viaud who was suffering greatly with Achilles tendonitis. I knew he was in agony as he winced with every footfall; I admired his tenacity as he was clearly in greater pain than I. About five miles from the finish, we joined up with Gérard Bertin and the three of us finished together in 11th place.

Halfway through the stage, I'd met Raife and Vik on their tandem; it was a great tonic, one that got me moving again, but they were clearly worried when they saw the swelling in my ankles and shins. We finished the stage in front of a wonderful *château* in St Georges-sur-Loire. Vik administered ice to my puffy legs, while Raife and I worked out an accommodation plan for them. After they'd managed to locate a place to stay, they joined us for our evening meal in the gym, and Vik gave me anti-inflammatories, massage and even acupuncture (for the first time in my life). What a unique first encounter we'd had!

---

[9] The main body of riders in a bicycle or running race, from the French *peloton* meaning small detachment (the etymology is the same as English word platoon)..

One piece of Transe Gaule folklore says: "If you reach the Loire, you'll see the Mediterranean." I was highly skeptical as I limped across the bridge spanning that beautiful river at the start of Stage 6. My shins were extremely sore, and they hurt with every footstep. Walking proved marginally more comfortable than running, but it certainly prolonged the misery. It was a very low point for me, as I drifted to the back of the pack. But at around 20 miles, everything started to improve. The pain got no worse; I was running more loosely and so naturally felt better; and I made up three places in the last five miles. I sincerely hoped that I wouldn't have to suffer through too many more stages with pain like that.

The next day was to be another "short" stage of 35 miles. Given my injuries, these distances were definitely easier on my head than grueling and interminable 45 plus mile stages, but the big psychological boost for me was to realize that I was one third of the way there! I sat at the finish line, tired and relieved, with my shins wrapped in ice (courtesy of a "bar raid" by Raife and Vik) and ate large quantities of *riz-au-lait* (rice pudding) donated by a kindly Transe Gaule supporter. I was starting to think that it was possible that I could make it to the Mediterranean, but I was certainly expecting a few more bad days. Interestingly, up to this point in the race, there had still been no "abandons" (people leaving the race due to injury, illness or psychological meltdown). By contrast, there had usually been four or five by this stage in previous years' races.

The pain in my shins and ankles was thankfully starting to recede a little, and I ran for much of the next day with Gérard Bertin. We finished together in 11th place again. We held off a late charge from Daniel Muller and Fabrice Rosa, who had teamed up with Alain Lemarchand and Christophe Midolet. This was a great result for Gérard, who rewarded me graciously at the gym in Monts-sur-Guesnes with a bowl of chicken noodle soup.

The evening was charming. We had a free tour of the splendid *Mairie* (a converted 12th century castle) which had also served as the location of the finish line for the day's stage, and enjoyed a brief reception with the mayor. By now, Susan had returned to her home in the south of France, and so I found myself in the key role of French-English translator. Normally, this would not have been too challenging for me, but I found that fatigue was really starting to affect my mental acuity. On several occasions, I had to ask for simple facts to be repeated so that I could make sense of them in English.

Sadly, it was Raife and Vik's last night before heading back to London. They joined us for a special dinner at the only restaurant in town which, while normally closed for the month of August, had opened especially for us. During dinner, the three of us had fun playing a game we'd devised called "Who are the five craziest competitors in the race?" It would be unkind to name names, but suffice it to say that two of the nominees were actually able to pee while running (you try it, fellas!) to avoid stopping and losing the 30 seconds or so that a pit stop would require. After all the laughter and support, I was very sad to see them leave for home at the end of the evening.

We entered our second week on the road, heading from Monts-sur-Guesnes to the spectacular Angles-sur-l'Anglin, renowned as one of the most beautiful villages in France, and rightly so. Every view of the village is worthy of a picture postcard. I finished in a respectable ninth place, four minutes behind Daniel Muller. I passed Sebastião, who was fighting demons – bad knee and foot problems – at about 30 miles. Janne was still the clear overall leader; he'd won every stage. Second was being closely contested by Trond, Bernard and Jan. Sebastião was paying the price for his early aggression and lack of conservative pace. Hiroko, the first woman in the race, lay in fifth. Frenchmen Laurent and Fabrice Rosa were comfortably ahead of me in the overall classification, and I knew that unless they developed injury problems each would be hard to catch.

To this point, there were still no *abandons* – it was amazing everyone, not least of all race director J-B. Almost 26 miles into Stage 8, we passed the 500km mark. Finally, we were all starting to see real progress and slowly getting there. And the next day would see us pass the halfway point.

But after eight stages of beautiful weather, Mother Nature decided to remind us that August in France is not always a joy. Stage 9 was totally brutal, with constant rain, cold and tremendously fierce headwinds. I managed to complete the 44 miserable miles in nine hours, placing 13th. Without question, this was the hardest day of the race. Due to the cold and cumulative fatigue, I felt ravenously hungry the whole time. Food at the aid stations (melon, dried apricots and bananas) just didn't do it for me or my appetite; I craved carbohydrates – and lots of them – but there were none to be had.

As I sat depleted and weary at the finish line in St Sulpice-les-Feuilles, a local official proudly informed me that the town had laid on refreshments for the runners. I was ecstatic until the kindly old gentleman took me to the back of his delivery van, where he offered me a single cookie – our ration of one per runner was presented to us as if it were enough to last us until breakfast. Oh, well, the thought was there!

Next we entered the hilly, lavender-covered Limousin region, which is unbelievably depopulated, even by rural French standards. The scenery combined with the wretched weather reminded me of an unforgettable climb of Ben Nevis[10] that Claire, my sons and I had completed a few years back. Howling winds and sheets of rain are fine to reflect back on, but they are not much fun at the time. But having reached halfway and facing two mercifully shorter stages up next, most of us were starting to feel more positive.

---

[10] Scotland's – and the British Isles' – highest mountain at 4,409 feet (1,344 metres) above sea level.

But as always, good times and bad times can happen very close to each other on stage races. When I finally made it to Bourganeuf the next evening, I wanted to erase that tenth stage from my memory because it was bad ... really bad. My ankles and shins were miserably sore, and almost everyone passed me. This was my very worst finishing position so far, ahead of only Sigrid Eichner, Jean-Hervé and Gérard Denis – 21st overall. I was forced to walk much of the last 30 miles. My legs were miserably swollen, and I began to have real thoughts of having to abandon. On arriving at our accommodations in Bourganeuf, we were greeted for the first time by depressingly cold showers.

As the sun was setting, I lay on my cot in the gym in a deep funk, feeling hopelessly sorry for myself. When Claire called my cell phone, I was about to start explaining why I was seriously thinking that I'd reached the point of dropping out. But before I got the chance, she interrupted me to tell me that an interview with Pam LeBlanc of the Austin American-Statesman had been scheduled for the Monday after I returned. Doh! How could I return to Austin and tell the story of being the only Transe Gaule quitter? Well, so much for dropping out.

The evening proved to be many times better than the day itself. The town managed to produce a friendly bar with nice cheese sandwiches and cold beer, a great kebab restaurant, and a pharmacy well stocked with ibuprofen (affectionately known by runners as Vitamin-I). We were officially welcomed as visiting celebrities by the mayor, and by the time I went to bed, full of beer, kebabs and painkillers, I was at last feeling better about my chances of survival.

So my trepidation as we started Stage 11 was understandable, even given its encouragingly short distance, 31 miles. The first twelve miles were all uphill, and the first two miles out of Bourganeuf seemed nearly vertical. But after that, I managed to get into a nice rhythm running with Christophe, Alain and Fabrice Rosa. We co-paced the last 25 miles comfortably and finished in 15th place together. Not a stellar performance, but much better psychologically than the last two days.

Our arrival at Peyrelevade was the very best so far. Kids asked for autographs and took our photographs; ice, beer and coke flowed freely; and a wonderful restaurant right at the finish line was serving *tomatoes farcies* and *frites*. It was an idyllic moment with beautiful weather and superb countryside. Without a doubt, I'll definitely return to Peyrelevade if I ever get the chance. The prospect of the next day's 48 miles was scary, but with seven days left, I was beginning to reckon that I could actually make it to the finish.

The next stage, 48 miles from Peyrelevade to Mauriac, was the longest of the whole race, but I was done in less than ten hours – finishing in 19th place – with a mixture of running, walking, and hobbling. It was a beautiful route across the Dordogne valley, which included a bone-jarring 7-mile descent followed by a wicked 6-mile ascent (which I didn't even try to run; I didn't want to push too hard, as there were still some serious hills ahead). I realized I was now two-thirds done. Better yet, the longest stage was behind me. All in all, I was in my best mental state since the first day of the race.

In Mauriac, I enjoyed a pleasant Sunday dinner in a quiet restaurant with Trond and Gérard Bertin while we discussed our apprehensions about another looming "climber" of a day we were about to face. Trond was very experienced, and on the way to his second Transe Gaule finish; he was feeling strong and confident, and went on to place second overall. For Gérard, this was his first major stage race; he and I were in the same uncharted territory. He would hang on to reach the finish in Gruissan in a commendable 15th place overall.

As we headed on to Aurillac, my legs started to improve. I was still experiencing tightness in my right hamstring despite lots of stretching each evening on my cot, but my ankles and shins were becoming less swollen. Even with this improvement, though, I was still taking a big dose of ibuprofen every 90 minutes, and needing to cut the front of my socks with scissors each morning to reduce the pressure on my swollen ankles.

Stage 13 got off to a strong start; with less pain in my legs, I actually felt like I could run again. It was all going so well until I got to the other side of the wonderful medieval town of Le Salers, where disaster struck. The Transe Gaule route was marked by various visual clues – chalk arrows on the road, pointers on street signs and ribbons tied to tree limbs. On a twisty road with multiple intersections, it was easy to let concentration lapse, miss one of these sometimes tricky clues and end up off course. And because the runners were so separated later on in the day, there was often no-one ahead to follow.

Well, I missed a turn and went three miles in completely the wrong direction. I did get to see a beautiful old church and a lovely mountain pass, but many folks got ahead of me in that stupid, wasteful time. This was nearly too much for me psychologically. Running further than absolutely necessary made me fuming mad, and it took me a while to calm down and mentally get it back together.

The course throughout the day was spectacularly beautiful. We climbed to the highest point of the race, the Col de Legal, at over 1000 meters, which positioned us for a long cruise down into the town of Aurillac. I made up some places after my directional blunder – four, in fact – and finished in 15th place together with the Swede, Matthias Bramstang. Despite my huge and costly mistake, it turned out to be a very good day with superb weather. For several days, I had been craving dairy products but was unable to find any at our stops along the route. I definitely thought our calcium luck would change when we finished in Aurillac where we were staying at the National Milk College. Ironically, at the very epicenter of the French dairy industry, the same was still true – there was not a fresh drop of milk to be had!

To give myself a little physical and psychological comfort, I managed to call ahead from Aurillac and reserve B&B rooms for the next two nights. I'd heard that the gym accommodations at our next two stops, St Cyprien-sur-Dourdou and Cassognes-Begonhès, were going to be primitive, and so I didn't want to take a chance for the sake of a few euros.

As each of the next three stages ahead was progressively shorter, it was definitely starting to feel like we were entering "the home stretch". Susan had rejoined the party with her husband Hubert, and we were all pleased to see her smiling countenance and happy disposition. I was especially relieved to be able to once again share the translation responsibilities with her.

Stage 14 was very hot with temperatures in the mid-eighties. The course had quite a few hills, but most of them were down, including an incredible 6-mile descent into the Lot Valley. With the shorter 39 mile stage, I felt stronger and suffered less leg pains. In fact, I even forgot to take ibuprofen once or twice!

Susan had decided to run this stage with us. From time to time, "stage runners" join stage races for one or more days, as training runs. They pay a fee for the privilege, and get to enjoy the same support as the rest of the runners, but of course don't get to place in the overall race rankings. It does provide a nice opportunity to run with someone different for a change. As the day began and we wound our way out of Aurillac, it was fascinating to compare Susan's bouncy stride with the labored plodding of the rest of the competitors. Thirteen consecutive ultramarathons had obviously taken their toll on all 24 of us.

I finished 12th in seven hours. I'd wanted to stay ahead of three competitors: Fabrice Viaud and *les jumeaux* ("the twins" – a nickname earned by Christophe and Alain for running and finishing every stage together). These folks were in the next three places after me in the overall rankings (like in the Tour de France, known as the *Classification*

General, or CG). I had gained some time on each of them, which made me feel I should be able to comfortably hold onto 11th place in the CG overall, but I hoped I hadn't pushed too hard on this stage.

I was entranced by this beautiful part of France: tranquil, little traffic, and full of nice, friendly people. Unfortunately, a rueful Jean-Benoît told me that: "France is dying!" These same villages that were thriving five years ago when he first ran coast-to-coast were now deserted or slowly being claimed by the British for vacation homes.

So on to the lyrically named village of Cassognes-Begonhès, where Stage 15 ended right in front of a restaurant which served delicious *côte de veau, frites* and cold beer. The stage's "Finish" sign wasn't up, as it was too windy; frequent strong headwinds had helped to keep temperatures down on our journey. It had been a 35 mile stage with quite a lot of climbing. Now that my leg pains had receded, I felt I was running more comfortably again, and had managed to stay in ninth place, ahead of two Transe Gaule legends: fellow Texan Don Winkley from Corpus Christi and Daniel Muller from Narbonne. Both these fine gentlemen have completed all seven editions of the Transe Gaule. Respect! I was definitely preferring shorter stages like this one, and now there were only three more to go.

My decision to book a room in a B&B turned out to have been an excellent one. Toilets, showers, sheets – I swore I'd never take these things for granted again. I felt embarrassed when I briefly visited the folks who were holed up in the primitive conditions at the gym, knowing that I had such luxury to return to.

After a great night's sleep and wonderful breakfast at the B&B, I was underway on Stage 16 as usual at 7 a.m. The run felt good despite lots of climbing; I had developed a new technique which seemed to work well – 50 steps running followed by 20-30 steps of power-walking on any and every uphill. While this may sound a little wimpy, I tested its effectiveness against Sebastiaõ, who was running continuously up and down the hills. I managed to keep up just fine, finishing ahead of him, Don Winkley and Daniel Muller for ninth place again.

We found ourselves running through such beautiful countryside. St Sernin-sur-Rance is where a young child in the 1800s was raised by wolves, and then discovered by humans. François Truffaut even made a movie about him – *L'Enfant sauvage*. To this day, the remote woods and hills surrounding the town preserve an eerie feel of desolation and menace, and so it was a relief to arrive there and rejoin civilization. We ran downhill for over six miles to the Tarn River; I felt a slight pain above my left knee as we descended, but my shins and ankles were relatively pain-free. The stage finished right at the *enfant sauvage* statue in the middle of town. I'd managed to book another stay in a hotel by the finish line – more luxury! Two long, hilly days of running remained. I knew I'd be desperately happy to be done, but leaving the *camaraderie* of this group of wonderful people was not something I would relish. This had been a unique experience in my life, and I was starting to understand why soldiers hate to leave their units when tours of duty end.

That afternoon, I was sitting in a café opposite the finish line recovering with some friends, when I saw someone walking towards me with a strangely familiar face – unbelievably it turned out to be Claire! This was the most amazing and delightful postscript to a long day of running. She had spent 24 hours flying from Austin via Chicago and Paris to Toulouse, where she had rented a car and then driven to this tiny village in the French back-of-beyond. It was the best surprise of my entire life, I swear. After a huge hug, I introduced her to everyone, and she joined us for a typical Transe Gaule dinner in the hotel where I'd booked a room. It was fantastic timing on her part. Now I had to call my daughter Tracey back in England to update my blog each day. We were all hoping our teenage sons back home weren't turning feral!

The penultimate day, Stage 17, was a long 44 mile trek with a very hilly first half. Having Claire as crew boosted my spirits greatly; it didn't hurt that we only had one more stage to go either. I was generally feeling comfortable but very tired, probably even more so than I realized. My left knee was sore on the downhills, but *pas grave* – not serious. I had a lot of fun running some sections with Claire, but I don't think she appreciated how weary I really was. She wanted me to get going and catch folks in front, but neither my flesh nor spirit was willing.

We ended up staying that night in a shabby, noisy hotel room right by the start line in St Pons-sur-Thomières. Already, I was thinking ahead to after the race and longing to spend a couple of days on the beach in Gruissan with Claire doing absolutely nothing except resting and eating.

A later start time had been planned for the final day

(7:30 a.m. – woohoo!), and everyone started the 18th and final stage in great spirits: more group photos were taken, and we sang several choruses of "*Vamos a la Playa!*" Many of us agreed to finish together on the beach at Gruissan Plage. However, there was still the small matter of the tough 43 miles between St Pons and Gruissan to be taken care of.

It was a very long, miserably hot day on the road until we reached the coastal area approaching Gruissan where, ironically, it became cold and foggy. I kept a struggling Sebastiaõ company for several hilly, wine country miles, before hitting some pretty but interminable stretches along the Canal du Midi. The canal is beautifully lined the whole way with spectacular plane trees, whose bark looks like camouflage; its flat towpath took us right to the center of Narbonne, a large city which thankfully J-B had signed very well. I started to bonk badly on the way out of Narbonne, nearly running out of water, but then it all came back when I found an unmanned aid station by the side of the road well stocked with mineral water and coke.

Two kilometers from the finish, I met up with
Daniel, Matthias, Fabrice Rosa and Roger. Claire
had parked her car and waited with us for the
arrival of Jean-Hervé, Gérard Bertin, Patrick Bonnot,
Alain and Christophe. When they finally came into
view, they were clearly happy but very weary and
ready to be done; we all set off together to jog the
last stretch through Gruissan. As the fog shrouded
beach loomed into view, we caught sight of the
finish banner surrounded by J-B, the race volunteers
and a few curious beachgoers in bathing suits.
When we reached the sand, with 100 meters to go to
the finish line, we joined hands, ran side by side and
reveled in the moment. We had all made it across
France – together. It was a hugely emotional and
moving moment for everyone.

In the midst of the celebration, Patrick hugged me,

shook my hand and called me a "true gentleman" for waiting and being part of the group that had agreed to finish together. I have never felt more honored in my life and was moved to tears.

We all took off our shoes and socks as we headed to the water's edge. Fabrice Rosa produced a tiny bottle of water he'd taken from the English Channel in Roscoff 18 days ago and carried all the way across France. He poured it into the Mediterranean, wearing a huge satisfied smile. Everyone applauded and cheered.

After a quick dip in the sea, Claire and I headed off in search of a hotel, which proved no easy task; we finally found a decent (although not very French) Best Western. The awards ceremony and dinner later on that evening were done in the usual friendly, charming manner of the Transe Gaule. I received my 11th overall award and finisher's T-shirt. Everyone was duly thanked, and the spirit was wonderful. I called Tracey to update my blog one last time, and then called my parents in London. I realized that the dream was slowly ending; now I had to return to "real life" after the amazing experience of the last eighteen days.

AFTERWARDS

At the time, this had definitely been the hardest thing I'd done in my life. Running injured is tough, and having to run 40 miles a day while injured didn't prove to be the best "rest cure"! I would've liked to have run more consistently and placed in the top ten, but it was not to be. Given the state of my shins and ankles for the middle ten days of the race, finishing would have to suffice as my achievement.

J-B and all the volunteers were simply fantastic – the run would have been impossible without them. And it would have been impossible too without the tremendous spirit between the competitors; everyone was pulling for everyone else and, later on when we'd gone our separate ways, I found I really missed my fellow sufferers. 24 starters, 24 finishers – a unique occurrence in ultrarunning. Little did I know then that I would get to run with a dozen of them again across Europe four years later.

The day after the race ended, I lay on the most comfortable bed I'd slept on in three weeks. My heart was beating so strongly in my chest that I could count my pulse – every pulse point throbbed and twitched as my newly enlarged heart pumped blood to my reduced body mass.

My shoulders, arms, chest and glutes had all shrunk in size. I didn't have a scale on which to weigh myself, but my guess was that my weight was down in the 155 pound range, compared to my normal 170 pounds. My ankles and shins – now dubbed "cankles" – were still miserably swollen, and my left knee ached. My feet were sore from minor blister and toenail problems. But other than that, I felt surprisingly good. My legs were thin, but strong and tanned. My face looked healthy, with only chapped lips to show for the journey. During the 24 hours immediately after the race, I ate and ate. Unusually for me, I'd woken up famished, and was driven to consume most of a large tin of pineapple without pause.

What had I achieved? It was less about what I had

achieved and more about what I had experienced. Suffering for 18 days alongside 23 foreign runners through some of the most beautiful countryside in the world is something I will never forget. The impending dread of starting another day on painful legs, the joy of reading the entrance sign to the town where the day's stage finished – these were the two daily counterpoints of life as part of the Transe Gaule. In between, there were hours (between six and ten usually) of running, sometimes smooth, graceful and easy, other times grim, monotonous, painful and hot. But every step – good, bad or indifferent – brought finishing a little closer.

For much of the last two weeks of the race, I had longed to stop, to be still, to rest. But now I had arrived. I had reached that moment. It was a wonderful thing.

After two days in foggy Gruissan Plage, Claire and I headed slowly homeward. I realize now that I was pretty shell-shocked from the experience of the Transe Gaule. I was very tired, my feet were still badly swollen and I had lost a lot of weight.

On our second day in Toulouse, we decided to go for a celebratory run together along the Canal du Midi, which was by coincidence the same canal that I had run along for miles *en route* to Narbonne. As soon as we started to run, the pain and fatigue immediately returned. Instead of being able to cover the joyful six miles we'd planned, I felt lethargic and grumpy and was clearly holding back my energy-packed wife. We decided that coffee in pleasant cafés and delicious four-course French meals would be a better plan for recovery than more running.

During our very first weekend back home in Austin, we competed with our sons in a local race, the Fila Relays. With two high school cross country "ringers" on our team, we easily won the family division. My legs, however, felt like concrete and looking back on event photos I can see that I was painfully thin.

Over the course of the next few months, I needed a fair amount of medical treatment. I had an MRI test of my swollen feet and ankles, which showed some stress fracture damage and went a long way to explaining the pain and swelling. I also needed surgery to fix two hernias that I'd caused by trying to manhandle a heavy hot tub in our back yard. I was forced to take some complete and probably overdue rest. When I was finally ready to make a first tentative comeback run after surgery, my planned route was only a mile long – to the end of my street and back. It seemed as hard as some of the harder days on the Transe Gaule, a strange and very humbling feeling for someone who had recently run across a medium-sized country.

While I was recovering and running less, I made my own debut as a Race Director for one of Austin's oldest races, the Decker Challenge. This gave me great firsthand insight into the complexity and stress of putting on a running event, which to its participants always looks simple – until something goes wrong! I was also feeling so much better physically that I began toying with the idea of running across another country. A race called the Deutschlandlauf had caught my eye – the German equivalent of Transe Gaule, but slightly longer and harder.

C'mon, how much harder could it be?

DEUTSCHLANDLAUF – 2007

"The great thing about athletics is that it's like poker, sometimes you know what's in your hand and it may be a load of rubbish, but you've got to keep up the front."
--Sebastian Coe, former British athlete and now Member of Parliament

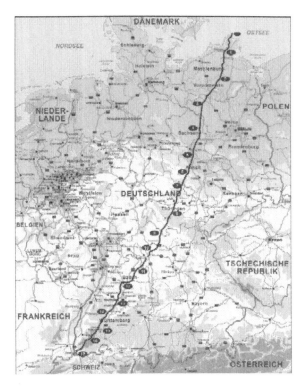

I and forty-one other runners from all over the world toed the start line at a place called Kap Arkona on the Baltic coast of Germany on a very cold, wet and windy day in September. Seventeen days later, only twenty-one of us would make it to the finish line in Loerrach, on the Swiss border near

Basel. Long, hard stages of up to 60 miles in the early part in the race resulted in many injuries which ended half the field's hopes and dreams along the way.

I already knew four of the runners from Transe Gaule – race director J-B, Hiroko Okiyama from Japan, Trond Sjåvik from Norway, and the German Sigrid Eichner. Seventy-five percent of the field was German; nine other nationalities were represented, including Australia, Taiwan, Turkey and Switzerland. Not exactly the United Nations, but a cosmopolitan mix at least.

The first week of the race was particularly brutal. Each of the stages was horribly long, the weather often wet, cold and windy, and the running surface was mainly concrete, cobblestones or rough paths. When the course followed a real road, we generally found ourselves running along the white line of two-lane highways with no shoulder, facing constant truck and bus traffic traveling at high speeds.

Each day quickly took on a very familiar pattern. We were woken from our uncomfortable sleeping bag slumbers at 4 a.m. to spend the next two hours washing and dressing, packing up our equipment, eating breakfast, and getting last minute medical attention for blisters or other injuries. Once the race got underway at 6 a.m., we ran the first hour or so in the very black and sometimes frigid pre-dawn. This was always when moods were at their darkest. Every seven miles or so, we reached an aid station along the course, offering a decent assortment of food, drink and mental assistance as needed. I found that I often struggled the most after noon each day, when fatigue and foot pain (which dogged me for most of the race) really started to take hold. My state of mind always started to improve when we got to the two-aid-stations-to-go point, with about fifteen miles left to run. By the time we reached the final town of the day where the stage was to end, the anticipation of stopping became a wonderful vision, marred only by the thought of having to get up early the next day to repeat the process.

Once across the finish line each evening, there was little time left except to shower, drink one beer (for nutritional reasons!), eat a large but often uninteresting meal, post an update to my blog, work with the paramedic on any new foot issues, and then sleep.

BEFORE THE RACE

As I got ready to leave Austin, my co-workers gave me a wonderful aid station themed going-away party. At the time, I was also coaching for Rogue Training Systems, and they sent me a "care package" of logo wear. I'd been sweating the arrival of one last pair of sneakers I needed for the race; luckily they finally arrived on a UPS truck the day before my departure. I left Texas in early September, spent a couple of days in England avoiding a perennial tube strike, and then flew to Berlin to meet Diana, my running friend from Austin who'd agreed to crew for me.

I had gotten to know Di during the preceding couple of years – she had worked for the Austin Marathon while I was president of Austin Runners Club. We had run together a few times, and her work ethic was always impressive. Most importantly for me, she was always a very positive person with an upbeat charm and ready smile – exactly what you need from any crew member. When I found she had free time that summer, I'd casually asked if she'd be interested in crewing for me in Germany. I was astonished and delighted when she said yes.

We met at Berlin Airport, picked up a rental car and headed north towards the start. We thought we were doing oh so well navigating to the Baltic Sea town of Stralsund, until we realized that we were on a very bumpy road with no exits, eventually catching sight of a border crossing in the distance. A quick check of the map confirmed that we had somehow made a detour towards Poland and were now incontrovertibly entering Eastern Europe. After some groveling apologies to bemused Polish border guards and some tricky reversing, we were given our passports back and sent back from whence we'd come.

Eventually we reached Stralsund, caught up with a few friends from Transe Gaule and met race director

Ingo Schulze for the first time. As we set up camp in the first of many gyms, Di had quite an introduction to ultra stage running – a line of participants standing in their undies waiting to be weighed and measured as part of a medical research study. Initial baseline data was collected from each runner, to be compared throughout the stages of the race. A collection of cups filled with urine accumulated on a bench, waiting to be tested later. It was quite an unusual sight for my newbie friend.

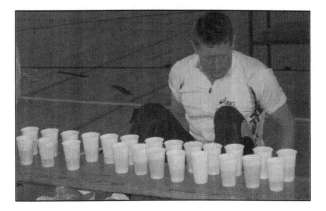

The kick-off meeting / welcome dinner in a nearby hotel later that evening was a charmingly confusing event – introductions were all made in German, and so the non-German speakers couldn't really follow along. I can usually get by in German, but apparently not well enough to understand Ingo's colloquial banter. But we all ate well, and returned to the gym to get some rest with a sense of anticipation for what was to follow.

THE RACE

The next morning dawned dark and rainy. After a very somber breakfast in a rundown, graffiti-covered school, we were bussed to the bleak, wet start line on Rügen Island. Does the name Baltic Sea bring to mind howling gales, freezing rain and U-boats? We had two of the three at our Baltic Sea start. Conditions were miserable until the last hour of the stage; I ran most of the way alone, but close to the finish line spotted my French friend J-B and we ran the final couple of kilometers together.

Di was an absolute trooper on Stage 1. (Remember … this was her first day of crewing, a twentysomething in a foreign country who couldn't speak the language and was surrounded by strangers.) Her role as my crew was to meet me every half hour or so along the course to make sure I had all the food, liquids and clothing I needed. Well, she had the misfortune to pick up a flat tire on our rental car early on in the day, but with help from our medic Jan Straub, the police, Hertz and a local garage, she managed to get it repaired in time to meet me before the finish. This was a traumatic start for her so early in the race, but she handled the situation brilliantly, confirming my opinion that she'd been the perfect choice of crew[11].

The weather was much kinder on the second day, as the course alternated between beautiful paths by lovely fields and deathly spells of running facing huge trucks and buses without any sidewalk or shoulder. Di ran some pieces with me, which helped raise my already flagging spirits. By the day's finish, I found myself astonishingly tired, after only two – but very long – initial stages.

---

[11] Some say that CREW stands for Cranky Runner, Endless Waiting. That just about sums up the sometimes thankless task!

By Day 3, I'd already lost three toenails and, for the first time, had gotten to know Jan, the medical man. Jan turned out to be an excellent toenail repair guy (as well as tire changer!). It was the longest stage of the race – 60 miles – and I was totally whipped by the end. But I was not alone. Due mostly to the very long early stages, ten folks had already abandoned the race. As the distances started to shorten a little each day, I started to feel a little better but my old friend from the Transe Gaule, foot pain, began to trouble me. And so I discovered the wonders of shoe surgery. Cutting away my sneakers' toe boxes immediately helped to relieve pressure on my toes and kept me from dropping out there and then.

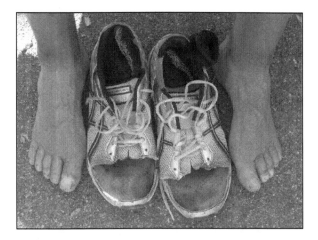

For the first time, the race doctor told me I was gaining weight – I'd gained a few pounds already, despite having run over 200 miles. I was about to learn that this was not a good thing.

As we reached the beautiful Elbe River during Stage

6, the number of dropouts had increased to twelve, despite shorter stages and slowly improving weather. Hilly terrain had now begun. We ran under awesomely huge turbine windmills, and were joined for a while by some very friendly local runners who were training for the Berlin Marathon which was only two weeks away. With my aching feet and very sore quads, I was just about surviving. And a little bit of black humor on this day: Di wanted to take a picture of me finishing a stage, so she met me a few blocks from the finish line. As we came in, I was in such sorry shape that I couldn't keep up as she ran next to me... and she was wearing sandals!

My weight gain was now increasing alarmingly – I weighed ten pounds more than when I'd started. My daily weigh-in with the medical team showed that my grotesquely water-filled hands, feet, legs and abdomen were expanding faster than my skinny, emaciated arms were shrinking. At this point, I did not yet understand that this additional "water weight" was caused by sodium deficiency.

The end of the first week was celebrated with a splendid finish line, replete with oompah band, sausages, beer and Germans. The weather was sunnier and less windy, and for a change I was running strongly – slightly too strongly, as it turned out.

Stage 8 was the day of misery I described at the beginning of this book. It was the result of cumulative fatigue, injury and electrolyte imbalance that nearly had me abandoning the race. I missed the time cutoff for the first and only time in my stage running career, but Ingo granted me a (slightly unwelcome!) reprieve.

I made the start line next morning, completing the relatively short but very hilly 40 miles very slowly – but at least I felt I was making some progress. Just before the finish, we crossed a huge, open field. There, right by the road, was an old disused checkpoint tower between what was once East and West Germany – quite a somber and spooky bit of history.

As the race went on, mornings grew more and more chilly – only 35°F (2°C) at the start some days – and I would feel the cold badly until the sun rose. We had made it into Bavaria, where the landscape was starting to become spectacular. Of course, "spectacular scenery" usually goes hand in hand with "wicked hills."

I was still frantically trying to find a solution to my increased weight and fluid retention problems. One of my fellow competitors was a Swiss doctor, Beat Knechtle. He was carrying out research into the effects on the body of these kind of multiday endurance events. His advice to me was to take in additional salt, as he believed I was sodium deficient. I did as I was told and started to see some improvements, but my swollen hands and feet continued to bother me when I ran. I was not however a lone sufferer. By now, only 23 of the original 42 entries were still in the race.

But with only a week of slightly shorter stages left, I was running better and ever more hopeful – though not 100% confident – that I would reach the finish. Di was continuing to get me through some very tough times. She ran a few kilometers with me each day to raise my spirits and always made sure I had what I needed – both physically and psychologically – along the course every 30 minutes or so. One night, I was still running after darkness had fallen. Di followed me in the rental car so that her headlights would light the dark, wooded pathway I was running along. I'm not sure I would've made it without her. By the time we "survivors" made it to Assamstadt at the end of Stage 11, we knew they had a good chance of making it to the Swiss border finish in Loerrach.

The next day, a blissfully flat course under sunny skies gave me my quickest finish of the race thus far. As we cruised into the beautiful town of Horb am Neckar, Ingo's hometown, we garnered B-celebrity status. Tents had been set up in the town square, music was playing and the locals were sitting on benches quaffing steins of beer, eating delicious food and generally having a splendid time. Ingo was addressing the crowd on a public address system as I arrived. He always liked to announce that I'm from Texas, even though deep down he knew that I was a Brit! But in just how many other sports do kids line up to ask a grandpa with skinny arms and grotesquely swollen feet in toeless shoes for his autograph? Where else would he be handed a microphone in the town square to deliver an epic speech in schoolboy German to rapturous applause? How bizarre, how bizarre...

With only two days left, we found ourselves eating delicious ice cream at the stage's finish line in the center of beautiful Sankt Georgen, which Di's research had revealed was appropriately close to the birthplace of the cuckoo clock. Later that evening, we pigged out at a local Chinese restaurant buffet, the first meal of the race that I'd describe as tasty. (Most days, our fare in Germany had been plentiful but rather bland – potatoes or pasta with some kind of stew being a typical offering.) The spicy flavors and variety were wonderful, but the poor waiters weren't able to replenish the buffet trays as fast as we could demolish them! So a great meal, blue skies and views of pine covered hills from our gym windows had earned this place the first 5-star rating of the race.

We were also learning the hard way that if our destination town's name ended in –*berg*, we could rely on a bracing climb to end the day. Feldberg, for example, was our penultimate finish, and it was certainly true to its suffix; but with only one day left, no-one was complaining. The scenery had become "Sound of Music" gorgeous, and the days were cool and perfect for running. My mojo was returning as my feet were almost pain-free for the first time in 2 weeks, and I was starting to finish ahead of some of the better runners.

The last stage into Loerrach was an easy 37-mile run down the Weise Valley along a riverside trail. I was finally able to run well, like a horse returning to its barn. I felt great and finished fourth – my best place of the whole race. My final ranking was 14th – I felt I could've made the top ten if I hadn't had fat feet for so many days, but so it goes. My two friends from the 2005 Transe Gaule, Hiroko Okiyama from Japan and Trond Sjåvik from Norway, clinched the first two places, thanks to great natural talent, steady pacing and super effort. Germans who had lead the race for the first few days cratered and either DNF'd or limped very slowly across the final finish line. As usual, this turned out to be "tortoise and hare" stuff.

In Loerrach, Di and I celebrated with sundaes at a local ice cream parlor downtown. I experienced the usual mix of emotions – elation at finishing, tempered with a tinge of sadness as things came to an end – but I was mighty pleased to be able to sleep past 4 a.m. for a change the next day.

AFTERWARD

Di, Jan and all the other volunteers on the course didn't just make finishing Deutschlandlauf tolerable, they had made it possible. I'd also enjoyed wonderful "electronic" support from co-workers, family and friends. Each day I got a huge morale boost as I read their blog comments and words of encouragement. It made a huge difference to my state of mind to be reminded that my progress was being monitored from afar ; a big and enthusiastic virtual audience makes quitting stage races inconceivable except under the direst circumstances.

Two weeks after heading home, I started to look back fondly on what had been a profoundly difficult and painful challenge. My feet were starting to heal and my body shape and weight returning to normal. Mental scars were healing too, so much so that I hadn't completely ruled out running Trans Europe which was still eighteen months away. Hey, how bad could it be?

Nuts, huh?

LAKE TAHOE ULTRA – 2008

"It's rude to count people as you pass them. Out loud."
- Adidas ad

In 2008, I coached a small group of Austin runners to complete their first Tahoe Triple. On a Friday and Saturday in late September, I crewed for them as they made their 26.2 mile daily journey at elevations between six and seven thousand feet. Thin air, long, steep climbs and little oxygen make this a very tough challenge. Because it is not possible to crew for the Triplers on Day 3 (as they run simultaneously with the regular, single day Lake Tahoe marathoners), I decided to run the Ultra, to serve as a tune-up for Trans Europe. This race starts at midnight at the finish line of the marathon, and the 72.2 mile course is the circumference of the lake. Just before the start, about 20 intrepid souls with headlamps and reflective gear briefly milled around before been sent off towards the "bright lights" of South Lake Tahoe, home to tacky gambling casinos and a few drunken late-night revelers.

My run started smoothly and easily. Each runner was supposed to have a support crew and vehicle, but I wanted Claire to catch up on some overdue sleep (she'd just returned from the UK and the birth of   our second grandchild), so I ran alone, hoping that the liquids I'd cached along the course during the previous two days were still there. Thankfully, they all were. I carried a small waist pack containing two peanut butter and jelly sandwiches, some GUs and anti-inflammatories.

Once clear of South Lake Tahoe, the streetlights ended and without light pollution the most incredible display of stars and galaxies came into view. From time to time, I turned off my headlamp for 30 seconds or so to get the best possible view. Words cannot describe the sight – a most remarkable five hours of stargazing. The lights all across the lake were a perfect man-made complement to nature's phenomenon. The temperatures never got below freezing, and there was almost no wind. In all, it was a perfect night through which to run.

Before 5 a.m., my cell phone rang. It was Claire, checking in on me. I was pleased to report good progress. I'd reached 20 miles – the top of Spooner Summit at over 7,000ft – by 3:15 a.m. and was closing in on Incline Village at about the 30 mile mark, still feeling strong as the dawn started to send the stars to bed. Suddenly, though, I started to have what are delicately described as "tummy problems." Each time I needed to deal with one of these little problems – at least three of which I can clearly remember – I would emerge from a port-a-john or the woods to see one or two of my competitors disappearing off into the gloaming, having passed me while I was indisposed. Although a little dispiriting, my system gradually returned to normal and I crossed the California state line feeling better with about 37 miles to go. One beauty of ultra running is that it teaches you patience and the need to accept the inevitability of fate while still pressing on. Eventually, I pulled back up to the folks who'd passed me, and I realized that by that time, many were in sorrier shape than I.

I had never in my life stopped during a race to buy a cup of coffee, but I did so at 8:35 a.m. on this day. I had been running since midnight and was by now at the 46-mile mark in Tahoe City. My goal had been to arrive at this point by 8:20 a.m., some fifteen minutes earlier, because my Austin friends were due to start their final leg of the Triple at 8:30a.m. But bummer of all bummers, I missed them by 5 minutes – in fact, as I arrived at the start line where I'd hoped to see them, the place was almost totally deserted. You would never have known that 500 people had just raced out of town. So to console my dejected self (and to refuel) I decided to pop into a bagelery and grab a quick caffeine fix.

My purchase experience was not a good one. As you might imagine, I was in a teensy bit of a hurry, unlike the lady being served in front of me who seemed unable to make a simple bagel flavor decision. So I waved my race bib number and asked the gentleman behind the counter if I might get a "quick" cup of coffee. "After I serve this customer…," he snootily informed me. While she continued to vacillate between poppy seed and cranberry, I grabbed a fruit smoothie and placed it on the counter. I was eventually informed that my purchases came to a total of $5.01. I had a $5 bill in my hand, which I hopefully proffered to my less-than-jolly, empathy-free barrista. "$5.01," he said again, pointedly. "I'll owe you a penny," I said, silently wishing bad things on him and any unfortunate offspring. His tip jar didn't receive any further contributions from this particular sweaty, sleep-deprived customer.

So, reluctantly, it was time to get back to work. Picture the scene: coffee cup and fruit smoothie in hand, disgruntled barrista scowling into my back, heading out for my last 26.2 miles of the race. Feeling a tad cranky, and looking out onto a totally deserted street, with not even a discarded GU wrapper or banana peel to indicate the recent presence of a stampede of marathoners. But I was fairly confident that I knew the way; I'd just follow the signs to Emerald Bay and soon catch up with some of the back-of-packers. I gulped down the end of my coffee (was it really bitter, or was that just me?) and started running again, clutching my untouched smoothie. A mile passed; two miles; then three. No-one. No trace of a marathon. Finally at 5K, I saw a marathon sign and asked two passing cyclists if they'd seen a few hundred runners. "Oh yes, they're way ahead of you!" they pointed out a little too gleefully. Finally, close to the Mile 5 marker, I started to catch the very slowest of the pack – a huge relief.

The next few miles were spent catching some of the slower Triplers as they completed their awesome challenge and the marathon walkers who still had a long, hard day ahead of them. There are some monster hills between miles 14 and 20 on this course, and the combination of 75 degree temperatures and brutal climbs was taking its toll. Slowly, I eased my way through some of the field and managed to meet up with my friends Carolyn and Keithly on the final approaches to the finish line.

I felt super-strong over the last 6 miles. By completing the first 50 miles in under 11 hours (actually 9:35), I had managed to qualify for the prestigious Western States 100[12], and I brought home a nice mantelpiece decoration for finishing fourth overall. This was my last real test before attempting Trans Europe; I was delighted that I managed to complete it feeling good, without the injuries and pain that had been troubling me for the last two years. Tahoe, while beautiful, is not for the faint of heart. It will always remain a highlight of my annual running calendar.

---

[12] The Western States Endurance Run is one of the oldest ultra trail events in the world and certainly one of the most challenging. The run is conducted along the Western States Trail starting at Squaw Valley, California, and ending in Auburn, California, a total of 100 miles.

TRANS EUROPE FOOTRACE – 2009

"All it takes is all you got."
--Marc Davis

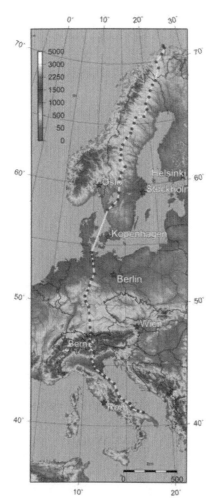

The Trans Europe Footrace 2009 started in Bari, Italy, on April 19th and ended 64 days later – Midsummer's Day – at the northernmost point in mainland Europe, the North Cape of Norway. The average daily stage was 45 miles long and no rest days were planned. Sixty-seven very experienced runners from twelve different countries had qualified to take part, each already having run a stage race across a country. A dozen of the entrants were women.

BEFORE THE RACE

Benvenuti a Bari said the sign at the airport – welcome to Bari, indeed! Three days before the race was due to start, I flew in to Bari from London, with a brief connection in Rome. It would have been much nicer if my luggage and I had arrived on the same day. It was worryingly missing from the baggage carousel – thanks a million to that hapless carrier, Alitalia. And this was doubly infuriating as they had gouged me nearly $400 in overweight charges. My bags were stuffed with six pairs of sneakers, a tent, sleeping bag, extra food, and clothing to last me the next nine weeks.

After a long wait at the airport to file a missing bag claim, a certifiably crazy taxi driver brought me to my hotel. He had absolutely no regard for any street sign, road marking or speed limit. Nor did he seem to believe that sharp cornering his minivan at 70mph was in any way challenging the laws of physics. I think I tipped him more as an offering to the gods for sparing my life than for his maniacal service.

With no luggage in sight, I armed myself with a

street map of Bari and set off on foot to orient myself
and to find the race site at the local soccer stadium,
the Stadio della Vittoria.   The town was a mix of
impressive ancient walled city and unprepossessing
modern construction. I eventually managed to find
the stadium where I met up with race director Ingo,
the medical team and a number of old friends – Jan,
Tomas and Helmut from Deutschlandlauf, and
Trond, Ria, Gérard and Nicole from Transe Gaule. It
was great seeing everyone again.

For my last stage race, Deutschlandlauf, I'd enjoyed
the support of a crew of one – Diana. Due to the
length of this race – nine weeks – I couldn't afford
the luxury of my own personal crew. Rental of a
vehicle alone would've set me back several
thousand dollars. So I was on my own – and at the
mercy of the race organization's volunteers. Finding
good places to sleep at night, lugging suitcases
around, shopping for extra food and medical
supplies – I'd have to take care of these kinds of
things myself now each day after I finished running.
Frankly it was not a thought I was relishing.

One feature of this Trans Europe edition was a
medical study which had been commissioned by the
University of Ulm in Germany and funded by the
European Union. We were to be accompanied by a
small medical team and an MRI[13] machine on a large
truck. My vital signs – temperature, heart rate,
blood pressure – and body fat were measured. I
donated blood and urine samples and then spent a
very uncomfortable and claustrophobic hour being

---

[13] Magnetic Resonance Imaging (MRI) is a medical
imaging technique used in radiology to visualize the
internal structure and function of the body using powerful
magnetic fields.

MRI'd. These were to be my "baseline" measurements against which my slowly changing body would be measured over the next nine weeks.

Foto: Helmut Dietz

After my tests and fond reunions, I headed back to my downtown hotel[14]. When I got there, my luggage was still missing and, with three days to go, I had only one pair of sneakers and the clothes I was wearing. But at least the hotel concierge was very helpful in trying to track down my luggage – full marks to him. The next afternoon, I received a knock at the door and was finally able to do the "big sigh of relief" thing – I've never been happier to see two suitcases and handed over a generous tip. As Joni Mitchell said: "You don't know what you've got 'til it's gone."

I picked up my race number and, like everyone in town running the race, I was raring to go. Our final welcome ceremony – a confusing, multilingual event the day before the start – was held at the swanky Governor's Palace in Bari and presided over by the head of sport for the region. Sadly it was the last warm welcome by a local official I can remember

---

[14] I had opted to stay at the Hotel Boston in Bari as an *homage* to the marathon which was just about to happen in Boston while I was in Italy. Oh, and it was cheap.

until we reached Austria.

THE RACE

ITALY

"And that is ... how (the Italians) are. So terribly physically all over one another. They pour themselves one over the other like so much melted butter over parsnips. They catch each other under the chin, with a tender caress of the hand, and they smile with sunny melting tenderness into each other's face."
- D.H. Lawrence, English author, poet and playwright

I stood at the start area with my fellow competitors and an assortment of spectators – family, friends and kids – on a dull, drizzly day in April. My PDA allowed me to post to my blog from the start line. I found it a wonderful way to keep in touch with folks back home and provide a daily journal of my travels and travails throughout the race. This was my first running experience in Italy and I was thrilled that we were finally underway.

The first day was a short stage of "only" 36 miles northward up the coast to Barletta. It was flat, the rain held off and the wind was mostly at our backs. The route was a mixture of scenic Italian seaside towns, ugly industrial complexes and long, straight country roads. As you'd expect, I ran slightly too fast – adrenaline and testosterone make me do stupid stuff. I covered some of the early miles with two runners I'd met during Deutschlandlauf, Mike Friedl and Hans Damm, but as they were both a little quicker than me, I wisely let them go at the halfway point and finished in the middle of the pack. Apart from the general tiredness and usual sore legs, I unusually felt like I was about to pass out at the finish line. The cause turned out to be very low blood pressure – the medics recorded it as 90 over 60. No wonder I felt like I was about to keel over! Apple juice and a few minutes sitting down got me through it.

At one point in the stage, a policeman stopped me and asked where we were going. I respectfully addressed him as *Signore*, described in my limited Italian the countries we were passing through and told him our destination, *Norveggia* (Norway). He was duly impressed and even drove past us later and gave a friendly wave.

Our first night's dinner was a total disaster. We walked to a nearby restaurant as directed, and all hundred of us piled in. The only menu choice was spaghetti Bolognese, and it took an eternity – well, over an hour, but that's an eternity when you've just run 36 miles – to arrive. And when you are tired and famished, all you want to do is eat and then sleep. Sitting patiently in a crowded restaurant watching inefficient waiters is not much fun, and we had some very cranky runners by the time food finally appeared.

It drizzled refreshingly for most of Day 2 and the temperatures were ideal. Much of the route was lined with miles and miles of vineyards, all bordered with spectacular wild flowers in full bloom. Austin prides itself on its profusion of wild flowers in the spring; I hate to be disloyal to my hometown, but what nature was displaying along that Italian roadside won out handsomely.

The toenails on my left foot were starting to take a pounding, despite running with the toe boxes cut out of my sneakers. Slightly tight socks plus rain were the likely culprits. This led to renewing my friendship with Jan the medic. Once he'd done his thing with needles and iodine, I cut my socks to alleviate the pressure on what was left of my toenails.

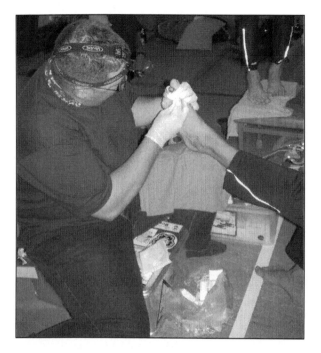

I got to spend my 54th birthday running Stage 3. By a nice coincidence, it happened to be Hiroko's birthday too and so we heard many choruses of "Happy Birthday to You" that day. This was the longest stage so far – 45 miles – and my legs felt very tired and heavy after 123 miles in three days. The day was rainy and windy, and traffic along the main Adriatic coast road, the SS16, was pretty ghastly. The police were very much in evidence. They cruised up and down with flashing lights, clearly unappreciative of our presence but completely unfazed by the prostitutes plying their trade every couple of miles at bus stops by the side of the road.

For the first time, we ended up staying the night in little wooden cabins at a campsite rather than in a school gym. A shower, toilet and bunk beds were a nice birthday treat for me. To end the day, my wonderful French friends from Transe Gaule 2005 - Gérard, Nicole, Jean-Hervé, Mélyne, Alain, Christophe, Roger, Fabrice and J-B – managed to conjure up a great birthday cake from who knows where, complete with candles. After dinner, they sang "Happy Birthday" to me one last time before we all headed off to our bunks for a typically early night.

We continued north. The terrain became more scenic and the weather stayed "runner friendly" – grey skies all day, but no rain. As we ran parallel to the coast, our first major climb was into and out of the town of Vasto. The race leaders were starting to really duke it out each day, with at least eight of them believing they had a shot at winning overall. Predictably, Hiroko was already holding a commanding lead in the women's field. I, on the other hand, was starting to get comfortable in the *peleton* and getting to know some new friends. My lack of Japanese was a pity as many of the Japanese runners were moving at similar speeds to me, but at least I was able to practice my Italian with bystanders along the way.

Not until five days into the race did we have what I considered a good evening meal for tired, hungry runners - antipasta, lasagna, salad, chicken and fries, and fruit (and wine for some). I was preternaturally hungry and gratefully ate and ate. It's amazing what a psychological lift food gives fatigued people. After dinner, I found a wading pool by the sea and stood in its cold water for quite some time, hoping to calm my hot, aching feet.

The hills continued, and the grey skies started to give way to lots of sunshine and heat as we passed along miles of seafront. It was tolerable for me, a Texas transplant, but others from colder climates didn't seem to appreciate it. It was not quite the summer season yet, so everything was starting up and not too crowded. Some towns seemed to be fine with this arrangement, but others seemed quite sad and desolate. The few tourists we glimpsed bundled up and dejectedly walking along the front seemed to be less than happy with their bad vacation timing.

As expected at this point, quite a few runners were starting to hobble badly with shin splints. Downhills were particularly aggravating for them and the terrain was starting to dish out plenty of steep ones. Fortunately my blisters hadn't gotten any worse and sensible, conservative pacing had left me uninjured thus far. At this point in the race, I chose to spend the nights sleeping in my small, lightweight tent whenever I possibly could. It traveled with me in my luggage and was quick and easy to put up and take down. I found it just as comfortable and definitely more peaceful than crowded, noisy sports halls.

As we made our way across Italy, the logistics of the race were still quite shaky. The line for the showers and toilets always seemed endless, and the speed of

Italian catering could never match the calorific demands of 67 runners and race volunteers. The night they decided to give us freshly made pizza – a great idea – was a disaster, as production was just not fast enough for so many ravenous folk. Some days we would be able to supplement our meager diet with purchases from local stores, like half spit-roasted chickens which we fell upon and devoured in the same way my dogs would have. These extra calories proved to be a lifesaver on more than one occasion.

After one week on the road, my feet were both pretty swollen and I'd moved up a shoe size. Each day my legs and feet felt good until about the halfway mark, when they started to feel tired and very sore. Jan had done a good job preventing infection in my two most blistered toes. His specialty treatment was draining blisters, bathing toes in iodine, then slipping a rubber glove over my whole foot before bedtime to keep iodine stains off my sleeping bag. I always felt honored when he photographed my blisters due to their uncommon size.

The best days were proving to be weekends and national holidays, when truck traffic was much diminished. Along the seafront, however, there were increasing numbers of vacationers looking for parking spaces, which made for quite a bit of dodging and diving. A week into the race, we had already had our first two "abandons," and more were expected as we had some increasingly long mileage days ahead.

The second week began with a very long stage, starting with some big hills into Ancona followed by plenty of flat stuff along the seafront into Fano. Most days, the weather was cooperating well – cool and cloudy – and there were strong tailwinds along the coast. Occasional heavy rains would blow in, seemingly whenever I pitched my tent.

I was eating well at the aid stations, which was helping me stay relatively strong. I concentrated on getting lots of bananas (to keep my potassium levels up) and washing them down with cheese and salt on crackers, tomatoes, apples, gherkins, salami sandwiches, peanuts, cake, chocolate, cookies, granola bars, apple juice and coke. Luckily, my dental hygienist Michelle had given me some heavy duty fluoride toothpaste before I left Austin to help combat all the sugar I was consuming.

Stages now were usually comprised of two distinct and completely different halves: very hilly, through some spectacular scenery just inland from the rocky coastline, and then flat with gale-force winds along the mainly deserted seafronts, including the resort town of Rimini. Both were draining in their own way. For our efforts, we were greeted at the finish a few times by gyms with cold showers.

Consecutive long days and hills were causing more and more shin splint issues, even amongst some of the leaders. During one final stretch, I actually overtook one of the top ten guys as he hobbled, cursing, to the finish. A few more competitors had abandoned and even more were expected to over the next two long stages.

By the time we reached Stage 10 – our first "double-digit" stage – we said goodbye to the Adriatic Sea and started inland up the flat Po Delta. Our first day away from the coast was blighted by three "police on scene" car wrecks. The first and most horrible one included cars, a truck and three fatalities. I thought the race might actually get shut down, but instead the Italian police directed us right through the middle of the carnage. Happening upon this tragic scene was a salutary wake-up call for us all. It put our lives, adventures and the risks we were taking into perspective. I've been hit by a car only once while running and I've concluded that I really don't enjoy running as a contact sport.

The course was long, flat, sunny … and very dangerous. One or two more had abandoned at this point for both physical and mental reasons. Some folks seemed to get preoccupied and obsessed by upcoming long stages, such as the 54 mile monster which loomed ahead, and that seemed to seal their fate. Abandoning was emotionally very traumatic; I could never seem to find the right words to say to folks who were devastated by quitting. Some were clearly happy that their torment was over; others were tearful and distraught that their dream – for which they'd worked so long and hard – had been shattered. A total of 22 runners would eventually abandon the race before the North Cape; I was good friends with at least nine of them. Reaching the finish line and hearing about one of those abandons was a bad way to end a long day on the road.

My blister and blood pressure problems were starting to abate, but my medical tests confirmed what I could see from looking at my hands, feet and abdomen – I'd gained a lot of "water weight" (5kgs, or 11lbs) just as I'd previously done in Germany. I spoke at length with the medical folks trying to solve this problem before it became a show-stopper for me. Extra salt and bananas hadn't done the trick so far and a Jenny Craig® diet wasn't an option; without sufficient calories, I would never see the finish. So I upped my salt intake further and stopped drinking Coke as the medics had recommended. Within a few days, my water weight was thankfully almost back to normal.

The route across the Po Delta continued with the "monster"; this long stage, at 54 miles, took me twelve hours to complete. At least the course was flat, comprised of a huge expanse of very fertile farmland which was once under water. After a nice, cool and cloudy start, severe thunderstorms built up in time for the second half of the stage. It rained a great deal and very quickly. It also left the narrow, two-lane roads covered in huge, muddy puddles which compounded traffic problems, as cars and trucks swerved to avoid them, each other and us. Lots of people including me were starting to look very much the worse for wear over dinner that night.

The next day started inauspiciously; cold, windy and rainy. I was very tired, just slogging through the first 15 miles. Then, suddenly, the day became amazing. The course headed onto a bridge...which turned out to be across the River Po. The river was a truly dramatic sight – at least half a mile wide and extremely flooded. Water and flotsam was flying downstream beneath us. As awe-inspiring as the sight was, the view soon got even better.

Our course took us along the towpath on the opposite bank for about five miles. Suddenly, off on the horizon, there rose the unmistakably snow-capped Alps. "*Es ist unglaublich!*" said my German friend Jörg Koenig. Yes, it was truly unbelievable. After nearly two weeks of toil to get to this point, it suddenly all seemed worth it. I still get quite choked up thinking about it. Even though we still had a couple more days before we would start climbing over those steep mountains in the distance, I would've been putting in the elephant order there and then if I'd been Hannibal!

It may be many years before I'll be able to face *rigatoni* again. Increasingly, our meals in Italy were tending to be interminable (when all you want is sleep) and uninspiring (it seemed as though all the caterers had heard that stuff about runners "carbo-loading" at pasta dinners – there was seldom an ounce of protein – or flavor – in sight!).

One thing I was starting to realize was that my Trans Europe experience had, for me, become a journey more than a race. I knew that if I ran faster, pushed for good times and obsessed over my middle-of-the-pack classification, then I would end up injured and abandoning, and so my conservative strategy seemed to be paying off. But what was happening in the race up front?

One great feature of this race was that the first dozen finishers from the previous stage got to start an hour later than everyone else at 7 a.m. Because of that, we got to see them scream past us each day sometime between three and four hours after our start. It was amazing to see how consistently hard they worked. Leading the race as we headed to the Alps were Rainer Koch and René Strossny, both from Germany. Early in the race, they both pushed very hard every day at an almost suicidal pace. I was convinced that at least one of them would eventually encounter major injury issues if this continued – and I was right. But now, for the first time, I was glad to see them starting to work together rather than trying to run each other into the ground. On the women's side, Hiroko continued to dominate but Ria Buiten from Holland was running well, too. These are amazing people I felt privileged to have gotten to know, but I wondered silently whether they were enjoying the journey as much as I.

As we worked our way up the east side of Lake Garda, we hit our official two week anniversary with only two days further to go in Italy before reaching the Austrian border. In those two weeks, we'd run an outrageous 575 miles[15]. The terrain was still flat, but we were all concerned that the mountains ahead would be a test of our legs which had become used to the "flatlands" of the previous few stages.

The scenery was now increasingly spectacular, but we were starting to encounter some fierce, draining headwinds. I'd started to take on more protein whenever I could to help with my weight and energy, usually in the form of salami, fish and peanuts, washed down with massive tubs of full-fat yoghurt. But getting enough of the right foods was always a problem across Italy. I also couldn't seem to get rid of a hacking cough. Many people in the group had developed similar low-grade illnesses, probably due to fatigue and unsanitary living

---

[15] Top Olympic marathon runners might train by running 500 miles per month. We were covering nearly three times that distance during the race. A recreational runner would typically take six months to run what we'd run in two weeks.

conditions. We spent our nights on dirty gym floors in sleeping bags – and in small gyms we were in very close proximity to one another. Nothing ever got really clean – not our clothes, bedding, plates, silverware nor even ourselves.

Much of the last part of our route to Austria took us along wonderful bike paths by the Adige River. As we headed upstream, traffic was either light or non-existent, but headwinds and temperatures reaching the mid-eighties made much of the day uncomfortable. Cyclists looked at us strangely, though they were often curious to hear about our route. Vineyards were everywhere, with medieval towns, covered bridges and castles littering the landscape, all framed by beautiful Alpine geology. It was my first time passing through this Süd Tyrol region of Italy and I was enormously impressed with it. As its name suggests, it's a German-speaking area, and every sign is a charming *mélange* of German, Italian and English.

Suddenly, some serious hills started. The last five miles into the beautiful, ancient town of San Michele were up, up, up. This was not exactly what the doctor ordered at the end of a particularly long stage, but I just kept telling myself that it was good preparation for the mountains that lay ahead.

AUSTRIA

"The situation in Germany is serious but not hopeless; the situation in Austria is hopeless but not serious."
- Old Viennese saying

I, along with 59 of the original 67 starters, made it to Austria. Italy had been a long (and, at times, very difficult) struggle, and reaching our first national border seemed like huge progress. We had to battle through a good number of very long, serious uphill miles before we hit the actual border sign, all of this in 35 degree temperatures and biting, northerly headwinds (see, I don't want to make this sound easy!). To compensate, the scenery was again beyond superlatives. The apple trees in full blossom were an amazing sight, covering acres of fields in every direction. Villages and the mountains beyond them were each more beautiful than the next.

Shortly after arriving in Austria, we encountered the most dangerous part of the entire race so far – a three-mile stretch of unlit tunnels, which we had to share with cars and 18-wheelers. We were thoughtfully issued reflective jackets before entering – nice touch, eh? – but this was truly the stuff of nightmares. Because of fatigue, I was having some balance problems. Remaining upright is an unconscious but complex process which uses muscles in ways we don't always realize. Running along narrow sidewalks within tunnels always scared me, as I worried that I might I lose my balance and totter into the path of an oncoming vehicle. Thankfully, I managed to stay on my feet and made it through.

Our second day in Austria was dominated by a seven-mile climb over the Reissepass, which took most of us at least two hours to get to the 5000 foot summit. As you'd imagine, many with shin splint issues suffered miserably on the long, steep descent. My cautious pace downhill had helped me avoid shin splints completely, but I was still wrestling with a cold. Despite some coughing, hacking and sneezing, I was thrilled to be just thirty miles from Germany and beautiful places like Füssen and Neuschwanstein which Claire and I had visited years before on vacation.

Our final encounter with Austria was a long, cold, traffic-heavy climb up and over the Fernpass (the place where, apparently, Hannibal's elephant concept went horribly wrong). By 8 a.m., we had reached the summit and were able to enjoy a more restful and sunny descent through the towns of Lermoos and Reutte.

GERMANY

"If I go to Germany, I learn something in addition. The German television is very precise and respectable. One has never stress. In Italy it is more dynamic. But I amuse myself madly in both countries."
- Michelle Hunziker, Swiss actress, model and singer

After a final thirty Austrian miles, we passed unceremoniously into Germany. There was no sign, flag or anything to indicate our arrival, except – and I kid you not – the world's largest wheelbarrow. I was too busy looking for a border sign and forgot to take a photo of the wheelbarrow. You'll have to take my word for it. Just imagine a really big wheelbarrow, and there you have it.

The remainder of the day was filled with flat, traffic-free, hard-to-get-lost-on bike trails, beautiful blue skies and stunning views. We passed through the lovely old town of Füssen, where tourists actually turned out and cheered for us, and then went on to the finish at the village of Seeg. A wonderful

Bavarian reception awaited us, with that lederhosen slapping / dancing thing, sausages and rolls and requests from star-struck kids for autographs. Now this was more like it!

As we pressed on through Bavaria, the weather remained good, the terrain was rolling but not truly hilly and the natives were friendly. The sports halls we called home every night were, for the most part, delightfully spacious and modern with fully functional hot showers. Like most of us, I felt very, very weary, having run 880 miles in three weeks.

Although at this point my pains were not getting worse, I had started to develop a worrying, unconscious list to the right as I ran. Some things – sailors' hats, for example – look good at a jaunty angle. Runners don't, though.

I think my body was trying to protect my injured

right hip, hamstrings and sciatic nerve, but it was a little freaky, especially because (a) people kept pointing it out to me with concerned looks on their faces, and (b) I was unaware of it until I glimpsed my shadow or reflection from time to time.

A lot of competitors were becoming deeply tanned from spending so many hours in the blazing sun. I always made sure that I was covered up when the sun was at its strongest and never ran without a hat and sunglasses. I made sure to steer clear of skimpy tops. The Europeans in the race didn't seem to have gotten the memo about the cancerous risk of broiling in the sun for hours. They wore little by way of sun block or clothing to protect against skin damage. Even worse, some wore no hat or sunglasses, despite research which shows the dangerous effects of UV light on eyes[16].

Though my "listing to the right" didn't get significantly worse, my back was becoming quite painful. I was concerned that my muscles were slowly wasting due to inadequate recovery time and poor diet. One look at my biceps confirmed this – they looked weak and wizened despite working hard all day. My back and core muscles couldn't give my spine the support it needed. What to do? Well, apart from just sucking it up, I could only continue to try to find more protein each day. As far as recuperation, there were no options there – rest is all I did when not eating or running. Lying flat definitely felt good, and I did so whenever I could.

On the positive side, the Bavarian scenery continued to impress. Everything there was spotless; even the

---

[16] Amazingly, one of the worst offenders was an optician.

cows appeared freshly bathed and seemed to be smelling of roses. It is a surreal corner of the world – litter-free, manicured and ever so slightly anodyne. I thought it would be an odd but very pleasant place to call home.

Over the next few days, my cold and cough improved, my listing to the right didn't worsen, and despite another mega-blister my feet and legs seemed to be working OK. The weather continued to offer nice temperatures and a mix of sun, cloud and gently breezes. The course was easy on the eye and quiet too, with less traffic, which was refreshing – running and playing "dodge the truck" all day becomes surprisingly wearing on the soul.

The number of abandons continued to mount with the miles of the stages, and at this point, 12 of the original 67 starters were now back home with loved ones. While I envied them their homecoming, abandoning would have been very tough, especially after having suffered for three weeks. One of the ways I rationalized my suffering and pushed myself to continue each day was to always keep in mind that there was a definite end of the race in sight – on June 21st. With three weeks now done, I knew that the six weeks we had left would eventually pass and would one day be over. It was chastening to remind myself that these few weeks remaining were much shorter than typical jail terms or military deployments. I had after all chosen to compete in this race!

Before the start of several stages, we awoke to huge downpours. Each time, as if by magic, the rain gods would relent five minutes before our 6 a.m. start, and we escaped with only intermittent drizzle all day. It was quite uncanny. I'm not a believer in prayer, but I could see why you could make the connection if you had a mind to.

We crossed the River Main at Würzburg, a beautiful old town I'd like to have seen more of if it hadn't been for this damned footrace. Just before we arrived there, a police car pulled up beside me as I was running on a cycle path. I'd never been pulled over by the police during a race before. I explained our journey from Italy to Norway, and once they'd made sure that they'd understood me correctly was sent on my way with a cheery wave. This could've been a dangerous approach – one of the other runners faced a similar situation in Northern Italy and was nearly hauled in by the cops, as the story of running to Norway sounded so implausible and – well – crazy.

I noticed two things absolutely everywhere in Germany – cuckoos and solar panels. I found the cuckoos to be charming; the solar panels unfortunately were not. While I applaud the "green" effort, they look simply awful on old, beautifully weathered terra cotta roofs. And because we were headed constantly northward, we got to see every single one of them, as they were all installed facing south. I'm sorry, but a 17th century half-timbered barn doesn't look good covered in grey panels.

By the time we passed the 1,000 mile mark on Stage 24, conditions had turned very wet, cold and hilly, and our overnight accommodations for once were, sadly, nothing short of appalling. I shared a 15x15 foot space with four noisy Japanese and three angry Germans. Man. The showers were apparently cold – I didn't even bother trying them – and nerves were getting pretty frayed (not mine, you understand!).

Unusually, four of the race leaders had gotten lost early on in this stage. The course was signed as normal with small (two inch) orange arrows stuck to road signs, but when folks run in a group, an error on the part of the lead runner soon passes on to everyone following right behind. The leader had obviously missed one arrow and had apparently gone a couple of miles off course before they all began to figure it out. They were certainly not happy campers when they finally caught up with the rest of the field much later in the day. "Steaming mad" would be a good way to describe a couple of them. And to cap it all off, dinner and breakfast were not served at our accommodation – we had to take a shuttle bus to and fro. That cut into our spare time and broke our monotonous but somehow comforting routine. Some were more unhappy with the necessary adjustments than others.

Moods didn't improve much the next day as we started off with 20 miles of very steep hills, but by lunchtime we had arrived at the old walled city of Fulda, passing through it on lovely, flat cycle paths. It was odd observing "regular" people again as they hung out in the parks, walked their dogs and generally got on with their normal lives, while we running aliens passed through. I envied them, as I was really starting to miss everyday activities – things like reading the paper, going to the store or watching mindless TV shows. We take so much for granted in our pampered lives.

I was, surprisingly, feeling physically and mentally strong at this point in the race. Some of the other runners were starting to negatively fixate about the long, arduous, monotonous Swedish experience ahead, but I just figured that if I made it to Gothenburg on the ferry from Kiel, I'd be glad I'd made it to a fourth country. And I was comforted by planning my "worst case exit strategy," which was to "jump ship" so to speak and take a ferry back to London if I needed to. My mantra had become "every step takes me one step closer to the North Cape." My secret, non-environmentally friendly plan was to lob my sneakers theatrically into the Norwegian Sea[17] – that is, if I actually made it that far.

With seven days left in Germany, my list to the right abruptly changed to a similarly pronounced list to the left – I have absolutely no idea what was up with that. Otherwise, things were holding together. Food had slowly but steadily improved, and my water retention problems and my cold had receded. I had started buying tinned fish as a supplement to the rations the race provided which I think was helping my protein levels and overall general health. As usual, I washed it down with copious quantities of yoghurt and my favorite weakness, chocolate.

At about this point in the race, I started to receive a lot of wonderful assistance from some newly acquired Dutch friends - Anneke, Ubel and Jenni. Ubel and Jenni were running strongly each day, usually finishing a few places ahead of me in the rankings. Anneke was riding the course on her bike, crewing for Jenni. She would pass me each morning with a friendly wave and a cheery "*Goedemorgen!*" After observing my weeks of lonely suffering, they

---

[17] I didn't, by the way. My "green" conscience definitely won out. And my fear of arrest for littering.

were all very kind to me, helping me to find prime real estate on the gym floors each night, even though it eventually got them in hot water with the race organizers. Apparently "claim staking" was against the rules, but while it lasted, it was a godsend – a reminder that we ultra runners are hugely dependent on the kindness of others.

The days wore on. On one particular day of contrasts, we suffered through a long and extremely hilly stage on many poor road surfaces with steep cambers[18]. My feet were wretchedly sore, my annoying lean to the left drew comments from everyone, skies were grey with on-and-off rain, and a 42-mile stage turned out to be over 44. But then, at the finish line, there was a happy ending – a German band magically appeared, bratwurst was in plentiful supply, kids asked for autographs, and the showers were hot.

My body was feeling very tired and beaten up after so many days on the road; I was having to work very hard for ten hours at a stretch to keep in positive mental territory. My mantra this – and in fact every – running day is "relax and float." It's what I focus on whether or not things are going well. Being relaxed is obviously critical for an event of this duration. And the imagery of floating is my mental reminder to make all my energy work horizontally, not vertically (i.e., eliminating the bounce that inefficiently uses a runner's energy). It

---

[18] We generally ran the whole race on the left side of the road facing oncoming traffic. Because of the camber of most roads, this put continual additional weight and stress on the left ankle, leg, knee and hip. I certainly heard less injury complaints after stages when we'd been running on relatively flatter road surfaces.

sounds a bit hippy-dippy, but I do like to keep pushing simple, positive thoughts to the front of my mind to displace the negative ones that try to sneak in.

We'd spent four weeks on the road and had made it to the Hartz Mountains, after which things started to get flatter. On one hand, it felt like we'd traveled so incredibly far – and we had: 1,200 miles (averaging 300 miles a week, a daunting number). On the other, we were not even halfway; but, as ever, one day at a time...

The Hartz Mountains saw two more experienced runners abandon, bringing the total to fourteen. Hans Damm (who I'd first met during Deutschlandlauf 2007) had problems with a high fever, and Theo Huhnholt withdrew because he'd just had enough mentally.

Rainer continued to dominate the men's race, while Hiroko was doing the same to the women's field. The leaders were clearly working awfully hard each day to keep their places. The strain was visible on many of the top ten runners, as they fought injuries and fatigue. Me, I was still quite happy to be doggin' along in the *peleton* – *"Langsam und bequem"* (slow and comfortable).

Our only "almost tragedy" came at this stage in the race in Germany. A car and a truck collided while braking to avoid one of the female Japanese runners who was running in the road. It was never clear just how far into the road the runner had strayed, but the net result was that a young girl in the car had injuries that required her to be taken to hospital by helicopter. This incident made the local paper and didn't reflect well on the race. I had been concerned that some members of our party weren't treating other road users with the right amount of respect and caution, and this incident confirmed it. Ingo did a good job at dinner that night telling everyone about the incident. He underscored the need to keep to the left at all times and threatened with disqualification anyone caught running on the right side of the road. The general consensus was that we had all "dodged a bullet" with this serious incident.

May 17th is Norwegian Independence Day, and for the three Norwegians in the group – Henry Wehder, Eiolf Eivinsend and my old Transe Gaule friend Trond – this proved to be a big deal. That evening I bought them beers as a gesture of international friendship and because that day's run had felt good for me – probably my best running since the first few days in Italy. The first 30 miles were flat and the weather close to perfect. I tried not to get carried away, given we were due another long stage the following day. The last 14 miles were along a boring, gravelly canal towpath into headwinds, so not much fun or fast running to be had, but so it goes. I had a song stuck in my head all day: "Thirty Days in the Hole"[19] by the 1970's English rock band Humble Pie, as we were on the eve of the thirtieth day of the race. Unfortunately, my joy at arriving was short-lived, as the accommodations sucked and the showers were

---

[19] *Newcastle Brown, I'm tellin' you, can sure smack you down*
Take a greasy whore and a rollin' dance floor
It's got your head spinnin' round
If you live on the road, well there's a new highway code
You take the urban noise with some Durban Poison
It's gonna lessen your load
30 days in the hole
That's what they give you…

ice cold. Was that any way to treat Norwegians on that special day?

We picked up where we'd left off the next morning, running all day along the footpath of the Elbe-Side canal. It's a modern shipping canal, designed for transporting coal and other big stuff inland. The locks are even more enormous than the huge barges plying up and down it. Running along a towpath sounds nice – flat, no cars, watery scenes – but as it turns out it's quite soul-destroying if you do it for long enough. It seemed to take absolutely ages to get anywhere. After the stage, someone said to me: "I had *déja-vu* fifty times today!"

Fortunately I had my Swiss friend Christian Marti for company, so the ten hours we spent on that boring canal towpath didn't seem quite so endless. Our arrival that evening in Bienenbüttel was unremarkable, and we were greeted at the finish line by a nice big hall but wretchedly cold showers again. By contrast, our arrival the next day in Trittau, a tiny town somewhere east of Hamburg, was the very best reception yet. As we entered town after 43 hard miles, we were met by a public address system playing our respective national anthems and groups of school kids holding our flags. They proceeded to lead us to the finish line, where a rock band was playing and kids were doing gymnastics routines. Free, abundant, delicious food, happy people, autograph-hungry kids and hot showers! Trittau earned the race's first five-star rating.

By this point, my feet were feeling better and my "water weight" had returned to normal. My listing had abated too and I was practically perpendicular. Blood pressure was back to 120 over 80. My only lingering discomfort and concern was a problem with the sciatic nerve in my right leg, which on uneven surfaces (and there were lots) would send pains shooting down my leg, reducing me to a temporary hobble.

One minor tragedy did occur in Trittau. I dropped my Garmin® (GPS) on a tile floor when leaving the shower. Its screen smashed, rendering it useless. Sob. Fortunately, I had figured out pacing and so no longer needed its wise data. Luckily, no harm ever befell my PDA, so blog postings, photos and phone calls could continue unabated.

We celebrated the halfway point with a blissfully short, measly 28 miles – the shortest stage of the race – and many of us were done by noon. We were even allowed an extra half hour in bed, and so we "slept in" until 4:30 a.m. It felt very good to have made it this far, but it had nevertheless been extraordinarily hard, and a huge distance still lay ahead.

By now, my breakfasts had taken on a standard form – two rolls with cheese, ham, salami and butter, two slices of bread awash with Nutella®[20], a bowl of cereal, orange juice, a banana and two cups of coffee. I would also snag an extra roll with meat and cheese for my "second breakfast," which I took somewhere around the first aid station. While not exactly a veggie or low cholesterol diet, it's what my body needed to get me through another day.

We made it to the ferry in Kiel the next afternoon and prepared to sail overnight to Gothenburg in Sweden. This meant that we would not have to miss a single day of running – no rest for the wicked! – but at least it provided a welcome change in routine.

It was hard to believe that so many of us had made it this far. Before we boarded the enormous ferry, we got to eat coffee and cake with the Mayor of Kiel in the basement of the *Ratskeller* (Town Hall). I was justifiably proud of having just completed my

---

[20] The Original Creamy, Chocolaty Hazelnut Spread™

second (and last!) crossing of Germany on foot. The final German stage had felt good for me – with little trouble from sciatica, a beautiful course, fine weather and hills that were not too steep. As we boarded the ship, the skies turned dark. Thunder and lightning started, and torrential rain began to eliminate any visibility. Fortunately, the storm subsided quickly, averting a crossing which might have become a vomit fest.

It had been an unusual day. In Germany, May 21st is Ascension Day, Fathers' Day and a public holiday all rolled into one. To celebrate, older people cycle around, while groups of young men in their 20's and 30's walk around boisterously with handcarts full of beer. I'd had this described to me, but I couldn't really imagine it until I witnessed it for myself. How bizarre. I wondered if we'd happen upon anything as strange over the next 25 days as we traversed Sweden.

SWEDEN

"I love Sweden. The entire world should be like Sweden. They all like to drink and get naked, and the women are hot. I can't think of a better nation on the planet."
- Drew Curtis, the founder of FARK.com[21]

After a monster buffet breakfast on the ship, we disembarked to be greeted by cheering crowds, cameramen and the press. They were actually covering the story about the two Swedish army guys

---

[21] Drew's first book *It's Not News, It's FARK: How Mass Media Tries to Pass off Crap as News* became a bestseller.

in the race (see Interesting Characters later in the book) but we got to bask in some reflected glory for a short while nevertheless. Then it was time to set out in the cold and pouring rain. Skies were grey and leaden all day, with some heavy downpours thrown in. Luckily, I'd grabbed my Goretex® jacket just before the start, which proved to be an absolute lifesaver. We left Gothenburg by bike path and followed nice, peaceful trails for just over 30 miles to a little camp of cabins. As with most vacation spots we passed through in Sweden, our cabins overlooked a peaceful but slightly ominous lake made dark by the peaty soil. My running was definitely starting to improve, despite the fact that I was working on cold #2. I found I was much happier with the shorter stages we'd had for the last three days.

At the risk of sounding like an ignoramus, the Swedish language appeared strange, impenetrable and at times absolutely hilarious to my English-speaking eyes. Many words read like Scrabble hands. My favorite direction sign pointed the way to *Lårje Hed*. Language issues aside, we did find all the Swedes we met to be delightful and friendly.

To celebrate the fact that we were officially five weeks done, we ran a very long stage (51 miles) followed by an even longer one (54 miles) the following day. Despite these exhausting days of more than ten hours on my feet – and still with a very long way to go – it did feel like we were making major, although very slow, progress. I found that my speed was marginally improving (see Nerdy Data later in this book). My only interest in speed was so that I could get done a little earlier in the day, which gave me more time to rest and recover for what lay ahead.

Our early days in Sweden typically started very cold and bleak but the rain usually held off and by midday we would often have a nice day on our hands. By now, it was already light when we woke at 4 a.m. I had no idea what time it was getting dark, but certainly it was sometime way past my 8:30 p.m. bedtime! The scenery was unchanging for days – gently rolling farmland with occasional villages, dark-looking lakes and streams along the way, occasional red barns and vacation cottages … and lots of Volvos. It was nice enough at that time of year, but I imagine that the winters there can be awfully long and depressing. And to make matters worse, there didn't actually seem to be anything to do. Yet all the locals we met along the way were very kind and friendly – they provided our cheeriest, best and most curious receptions yet.

By the time we arrived for the night at the inappropriately named Hassle Sporthall, at least five of the top ten runners were nursing bad knee or shin problems. Back in the *peleton* (where I was comfortably in 35th position at this point), there was a lot of fatigue, as each "long" day was taking an interminable time to complete. I noted in my journal that "my sciatica and feet were better; my Achilles tendons were worryingly sore for the first time; my quads and back was very tired; and I was very congested with cold symptoms. So … good for another 43 miles tomorrow!"

Things started to get mind-numbingly repetitive as we began to run exclusively along the shoulder of the main E26 highway for three days solid, until we reached Mora. Then we switched to the E45 for two more <u>weeks</u> of the same. The E45 is known as the *Inlandsvägen*, the major inland south to north two-lane highway in Sweden. Much of the time, these roads really did seem to go on forever – the buses and logging trucks barreling towards us certainly did. We were just hopeful that traffic would lighten as we got further north.

Stage 38 proved to be a very special day, despite having to run the equivalent of two marathons. At just over halfway through the stage, I was met by my Austin friend Mike who was in Sweden on vacation, visiting his Swedish family and running the Stockholm marathon the following Saturday. He chose to celebrate this special day – his birthday – by persuading his father to drive several hours from Stockholm to meet me on the E45.

Finding us wasn't too difficult as by midday we were strung out along nearly ten miles of very straight road. When Mike finally saw me, he jumped out of his father's car and started to video me with his Flip™ camera. He then proceeded to run with me for the next two hours, chatting about recent events in Austin and around the world which I'd been out of touch with for the past five weeks. It buoyed my spirits no end. To make things even finer, he left me a wonderful care package, replete with loads of fresh salmon and other high protein comestibles like beef jerky and macadamia nuts, a replacement Garmin® from Claire and a ton of well-wishing cards from family and friends back home. I was sorry that Mike had to leave so soon but at least he'd found me in good spirits and running well enough. Thankfully I looked in decent mental and physical shape in the video clips he posted to YouTube afterwards.

The fortieth stage was memorable for providing us with the most inhospitable weather to date. The forecast was, let's just say, off the mark. It called for light breezes, some sun and temperatures in the 60's. What did we actually get? Torrential rain all morning, bitterly cold headwinds all day and a fair bucket-load of hail after lunch. Fortunately, I'd kept my Goretex® jacket at the start; even with it, I was only a couple of degrees north of hypothermia. It was then that I reminded myself to always ignore forecasts and dress warmly. At least I fared better than some who took the T-shirt option that miserable morning. Fortunately, the next day's beautiful weather almost made up for the previous day's misery – cold and sunny early, then just sunny blue skies until about 2 p.m., when it clouded over.

The course along the E45 was littered with continuous and often very steep hills. Weekends were always much nicer than weekdays, which were filled with logging trucks pushing us off the road. As we got further north, sometimes we would go twenty minutes without seeing a house or even a vehicle. It was almost spookily desolate. Strip logging is the only real industry there. Apart from that, there's nothing except vacation cottages, lakes and rivers. It might sound idyllic, but it was almost morbidly quiet. In some parts, there weren't even stores or cafés. I can't imagine what teenagers on vacation with their parents would make of it. I generally felt good for the first 30 miles each day, but the last 20 made me very weary as the uphills and downhills took their toll on hamstrings and quadriceps respectively. One priceless quote from a non-English speaker: "I run easy today...I can feel my hamsters already."

Rainer Koch and Hiroko Okiyama continued to dominate the men's and women's races with six weeks complete. They pushed hard each and every day, even though that intense effort could have lead to injury and even potential withdrawal. Most of the rest of us were just busy trying to stay healthy (there was a nasty bout of bronchitis going around; at night the gym sounded like a consumption ward) and preparing mentally for some very long stages ahead. We all realized that there was still plenty of time for "the wheels to come off." One of the top ten guys – Cor Westhuis from the Netherlands – was suddenly stopped in his tracks due to major knee problems and forced to withdraw. It was heartbreaking, as this would've been his second European transcontinental crossing[22].

Stage 43 was a long, hot stage. 54 more miles of the E45, and it was very warm even as we started off at 6 a.m. Temperatures reached up into the 80s, with no significant shade or clouds along the way. The very best thing psychologically about Stage 43 (and you'll have to take my word for it that it is very hard to stay gung-ho and motivated after so much toil and so many miles) was that this was the last day of May. Every one of the remaining 21 days of the race would actually be in June, which somehow made me feel like we were closing in on the finish. This is the kind of crazy stuff you think about *ad naseum* on the road.

---

[22] Eight runners did make it across Europe for a second time in 2009, and deserve a very honorable mention: Robert Wimmer, Martin Wagen, Janne Kankaasyrjä, Hans-Jürgen Schlotter, Joachim Hauser, Werner Selch, Tsuyoshi Sugawara and Yasuo Kanai.

On June 1, we passed the 3,000 kilometer mark (1,860 miles) – a major milestone for most of us who had never run that far in our lives before. Balloons and the mayor of the *kommun*[23] were there to mark the occasion. After a quick break, we were soon back to work. The road was not too hilly and the sun was not too strong; blustery headwinds were the only negative. Off in the distance to the west we could see snow-capped mountains again. I awoke at midnight and it was still light. And we were still many miles from the Arctic Circle.

The next stage to Lit was a good one for me. The route took us off the E45 for most of the day, and instead of the monotony of the highway, we passed along the shores of a gorgeous lake with mountains beyond. We crossed the lake by means of a massive road bridge into the town of Östersund, which is the geographic center of Sweden. It's also where the national cross-country ski team is based, and we saw them practicing on roller skis in a huge training and racing facility on the edge of town. We'd officially crossed over into the north of Sweden. The weather was as Mark Twain described New England's – if you don't like it, just wait a few minutes! We had biting headwinds, strong tailwinds, sun, rain, hail, clouds – in fact, everything but snow.

Our evening in Lit was music filled. While we ate dinner, kids from the school played rock music on stage for us – the girl singers were really quite good. Then, as we got ready for bed in the gym, a relative of one of the Norwegian runners started playing guitar and singing folk songs...and then switched to

---

[23] The 290 municipalities of Sweden (*kommun*) are organized into 21 counties (*Län*).

belting out some great Janis Joplin. She had a great blues voice and for a few minutes it almost felt like I was back in Austin.

A week away from the Arctic Circle, the weather turned from unseasonably warm to unseasonably cold. I layered up and even wore Goretex® ski gloves, but biting northerly headwinds, hail and even a little snow made for a number of very testing and at times bitterly cold stages. One of the Japanese guys ran in a T-shirt and survived – I was bundled up and almost hypothermic – I just don't get it! During the course of the race, some runners clearly lost more weight than others. The medical team has not yet published its data, but my guess is that the average weight loss was about ten pounds. That's how much lighter I was when I arrived home. I do know that one competitor – the "biggest loser" – dropped nearly thirty pounds over the nine weeks.

Another milestone came as we officially entered Lapland. There were no reindeer or people in funny outfits, but at least there was a really big carved wooden sign by the side of the road. Now it truly felt like we were way up north! To give you a sense of how cold the weather had become, one aid station had splurged and put up Christmas decorations – a nice touch! – and we were delicately informed that snow was in the forecast. The one positive thing about this unusual cold spell was that it delayed the onset of mosquito season, a miserable time in Scandinavia (and especially miserable for me, as I seem particularly attractive to the little monsters).

Despite the progress we'd all made, a number of serious injuries were continuing to surface even this late into the race. Two of the top five in the women's race were battling terrible problems which made running very difficult for them both. The leader, Hiroko, was suffering from major muscle problems in her right quadricep, and Jenni de Groot was reduced to walking due to very painful hip issues. Tears of pain and frustration were in evidence from them every evening. It was very hard to know what to say to them, especially after they'd worked so hard and come all that way. Sadly, they both ended up having to abandon before we reached the North Cape.

A treat was in store for us as we completed seven weeks. We discovered that our accommodation one night was to be...a hotel! Only three of us sharing a room with its own hot shower and toilet. Pure luxury. This offset some of the misery of the day, which was again very cold, with rain, sleet and snow thrown in from time to time. Between my circulation problems[24] and my absence of body fat, I was really struggling with the cold. Despite being heavily dressed, I just couldn't manage to warm up. Even running harder didn't make me warm. My only option was to grit my teeth and push on. There were rumors circulating that the weather would improve in upcoming days, but I'd become increasingly skeptical about such "news". After all, "Arctic Circle" and "heat wave" seldom appear together.

Two unexpected things I saw lots of in Sweden were

---

[24] I suffer from Raynaud's disease in my fingers, a condition that causes them to feel numb and turn white then blue in response to cold temperatures.

vintage American cars in wonderful condition and trampolines (there's one in almost every other yard). I swear I wasn't hallucinating – they were everywhere. It's odd what you notice when you have plenty of time to reflect.

The eighth week started with some very long stages, including the race's longest day of over 60 miles. These would have been hellacious distances on fresh legs – in our weary state, they were really daunting. I had started running more with my Dutch friend Ubel Dijk. He's a former 24-hour champion of Holland, so I generally had to work a bit too hard to keep up with him. We were mourning the loss of Jenni de Groot, who had finally had to abandon after developing a really serious and painful stress fracture in her hip socket. She was a very kind, strong lady, and it was very sad that she was forced to stop after so long.

"Only two weeks to go" sounds much easier than the reality of the distance and conditions that were ahead for us ... but the problem could only be tackled one day at a time. As the summer weather worsened, so did our spirits. Black humor abounded – for example: "How do you know it's summertime in Lapland? It only snows once a day." Yes, it snowed most days – but rain and headwinds had subsided for the time being at least.

One night, I slept very badly due to raging heartburn, which lasted well into the first half of the next day's stage. I discovered a couple of other folks complaining of similar symptoms, so maybe it had been something we'd eaten for dinner? Thankfully the problem went away as fast as it had appeared, but incidents like this makes people very jittery during long stage races – there's a very real fear that some nasty bug will run amok through our weakened immune systems and force us out of the race.

By now, I was almost always running alone each day – through choice. I found that at this point I hadn't much to say and neither did anyone else this far into the race. So most of the time I preferred my own company, dwelling in my own thoughts, and choosing not to risk being brought down by others' negativity. I also wanted to make sure that I was running at my own speed – neither too fast nor too slow. On many days we were spaced so far apart that I didn't see another runner after aid station #1 until I crossed the finish line. Thus I was all alone when I glimpsed my first big herd of reindeer about fifty yards off the road. It was quite a thrill. The landscape had become more dramatic and interesting – implying, of course, hillier – but with reasonable weather, it was nice to gaze upon.

Our longest day on the road came at this point – a killer day of 95km (over 60 miles) which took me nearly 13 hours. There was rain at the start, then lots of sun followed by heavy rain and hail to finish off the day. I'd luckily remembered to never hand over my Goretex® jacket at aid stations just because the sky was currently blue. I also used my mosquito repellent for the first time, as they were just coming to life in a big way. There were many very tired people in the gym that particular night.

The scenery was very fine and traffic much reduced but despite that there were some very long, straight grinds back along the E45 – miles long at times – which were hard on the brain. My chances of making it to the North Cape were gradually improving with each passing day. A big psychological hurdle was overcome about five miles before a stage finish in Jokkmokk, where we crossed the Arctic Circle. A Scotsman and I took turns taking each other's photos in front of the Visitors' Center. The irony of my photo is that it shows me wearing a singlet and shorts. After freezing further south, we had suddenly hit nice temperatures at the Arctic Circle. Go figure. Even here, the mosquitoes were out in force too, but my repellent was thankfully working well.

The next day we faced another daunting 60-miler to the town of Gällivare; once we'd got past that, the final ten day countdown could begin. According to Wikipedia: *"The inhabitants of Gällivare have a remarkably high incidence of congenital insensitivity to pain, an extremely rare disease (which) prevents the sensation of pain, heat and cold. There have been nearly 40 reported cases in Gällivare."* I wondered if we'd get any temporary benefit from this phenomenon!

Gällivare is a major iron mining center. One of its workings, located right under an old and heavily populated section of town, collapsed a few years back. What has been put in its place since is not very prepossessing. I confess that I, along with everyone else I spoke to, was more than ready to be done; there were too many hours alone on the road each day, too many times when your mind turned too easily to missed loved ones and creature comforts. On this day, for instance, we passed through only one small town, comprised of maybe a dozen houses. That was it. This really was "the back of beyond." The fact that the day started with plenty of rain, then heavy, grey skies and finally ended with a huge downpour that sucked any fun out of the last hour did nothing to help our moods.

Throughout the race, we were wonderfully supported by aid stations about every 6 miles. Reaching each one made me feel as though good progress had been made. The volunteers were marvelous at these little setups, and drinks were plentiful, but the food became repetitive and uninspiring. I was becoming more concerned about eating the perishables, whose freshness was dubious without the benefit of refrigeration, so I stuck mainly to cookies, chocolate and cake to get the calories I needed. Not too balanced a diet, and after this many days, not really as tempting as it might sound!

My feet remained extremely sore, but they only needed to hang on for ten more days. The doctors operating the MRI machine traveling with us diagnosed them as "very inflamed but no structural damage." But seriously – ouch! They were miserably painful.

On route to the town with another Scrabble-hand name, Svappavaara, there was bad news. Following a day of rain, a strong, cold headwind, and surprisingly heavy traffic, two more folks had had to abandon: Mike Friedl, who had fought leg injuries since we arrived in Sweden and finally couldn't continue, and Fabrice Viaud, who had developed a staph infection in his hand and had been hospitalized for surgery. It was devastating for these guys after making it so far, and now only 47 of the original 67 were still in the race. The good news was that this was a much lower dropout rate than either I (70%) or Ingo (50%) had estimated.

We found out the next day that Fabrice's staph infection was in fact extremely serious. He immediately had one surgery in Gällivare to insert antibiotic implants in his finger and was waiting for a second surgery later in the week to remove those implants. In the process, they had to cut away small parts of his finger; so serious was the infection that a day or two's delay could've been life threatening. I'm glad to report that he has made a full recovery and is back to running again in France.

After a total of 57 days into the race, 24 of those in Sweden, we finally made it to the Finnish border. Though we were close, finishing was still not guaranteed, even this late into the race. Jörg Koenig felt unwell and had extremely high blood pressure early in the stage to Karesuando, was taken by ambulance to hospital and forced to abandon the race. It was Jörg, now so sad and disappointed after so much distance traveled, with whom I first spotted those "*unglaublich*" Alps weeks ago in Italy.

For a change, I ran much of the day with my Swiss friend, Christian Marti. Things started well, but we got dismally soaked for the last ten miles and I became quite hypothermic. Our good fortune was that Christian's wife Ursula met us at the finish line and drove us both to their hotel, where I was able to get a room for the night. I became deliriously happy with my own hot shower, a jumbo-sized bag of potato chips, and naptime in clean sheets....aaaaaah!

Our evening meal at a local church was even better. When I saw dinner set out before our endless line of hungry runners, I jokingly said: "Looks like we're having reindeer lasagna." It was in fact just that. And delicious. The rich meat and carbs were appreciated all round – it was part of a perfect multiday running diet.

The food and the people in Sweden were absolutely great. But the dismal weather, absence of wildlife (except mosquitoes), and the apparent lack of anything much to see or do left it low on my list of "places I want to go back to." My expectations for Finland and Norway were not set any higher, but I was definitely looking forward to seeing them both.

FINLAND

"(Our game software development company) Digital Chocolate has 60% of its developers in Finland where the sun never sets in the summer and there is nothing to do outside in the winter, so we are very productive!"
- Trip Hawkins, Digital Chocolate CEO

Ah, Finland! Home of Nokia and, well, Finns. My friend Mike from Austin was right – the Finns manage to string together more letters in their place names than even the Swedes do. Spelling tests in school must consume reams of paper...but I digress.

Our departure from Sweden started inauspiciously with a torrential downpour of rain during breakfast. This was no light shower. We started the race on the Swedish side of a river, crossing immediately into Finland. The rain poured, the wind howled and then thunder and lightning started to boom and flash. Everyone was cold and drenched; it was sheer bloody misery for the first two hours.

Gradually it eased up, and as we left the main highway to cross a mountain range via a smaller road, the skies turned blue and the sun put in a very welcome appearance. Today's bombshell was that women's race leader Hiroko had finally abandoned. Bad leg problems had had her hobbling for days, and finally she was forced to quit. This was made even more heartbreaking by the fact that she had also had to abandon in the 2003 edition of this race after 44 days of racing. Again, this was so late in the game for her to have to drop out; she was being a trooper, but was clearly devastated by having to withdraw, especially because she was holding a huge lead over second place on time[25].

NORWAY

"One day you are happy and laughing and the next you are crying."
- Grete Waitz, Norwegian running superstar, on her battle with cancer

With Finland done, we moved seamlessly into Norway, our very last country. It felt very good to reflect on that fact. But before we could get too smug, 51 miles had to be covered, with fierce, very cold northerly headwinds accompanied from time to time by heavy rain. Lucky for us it was summertime, eh? It was one of those "I just want to be done" days.

One thing I noticed when we got to Norway – there were no more pine trees, just sparse woods of silver

---

[25] Hiroko stayed with the race until the North Cape, working enthusiastically as a volunteer at aid stations every day, where she did an amazing job supporting and encouraging us all. Mike Freidl and Christophe Midelet had done the same earlier in the race when they had been forced to abandon. Kudos to them all.

birch. The landscape was becoming more mountainous and rugged as we move towards tundra and fjord country. Rivers were slowly taking the place of lakes in the scenery. I feared that there would be some serious hills and cold weather ahead.

My "Bridget Jones Diary" journal entry for my first day in Norway: "Wildlife - no reindeer, but one husky who ran 5 miles with me; Cigarettes - none; Alcohol - one alcohol-free beer to wash down my jar of pickled herring at the finish (protein, you know).."

The Norwegians we met seemed as delightful and friendly as their Swedish and Finnish counterparts. I was interviewed for the local radio station by a beautiful and intelligent young lady, whose command of English outdid mine after eight weeks on the road. Then after dinner we were treated to a bout of "yoikking" by two other delightful young Norwegian ladies. "Yoikking" is a cool Norwegian folk tradition, a combination of singing, drumming and chanting.

With four days left, I calculated that I had just completed my 100th Ultra - small potatoes for some of the hardcore folks in the race, but still a decent count (or crazy, depending on your point of view). This is the kind of stuff you think about when you have serious time on your hands and nothing of substance to fill your mind.

Despite the length of the stage (over 53 miles) and some nasty truck and trailer traffic from time to time, this was absolutely the best day of the whole journey. It started with sunshine, nice running temperatures and gentle breezes, but unlike other previous more changeable days, the great weather lasted all day. The run started out along a beautiful, wide river with barren, stony, snow-covered hills beyond. We encountered several herds of reindeer, one of which decided to run alongside us for a while. Then the river (and our road) headed down a steep gorge for many spectacular kilometers, and we got to watch the white water do its thing.

But as we approached the fairly sizeable city of Alta after about 30 miles, things started to change. Pine trees reappeared, farms sprang up, and the microclimate suddenly became alpine. Flowers and the smell of mown grass scented the air, and we were running comfortably in shorts and T-shirts. And in the distance beyond Alta was the Norwegian Sea, framed by fabulous, massive, ice-covered fjords. Even the Norwegians in the group were blown away – it was spectacular. Our accommodations in a school in the village of Rafsbotn just beyond the town were again "five star" – with hot showers, super-friendly hosts and very good food.

We had learned by now to expect that the good days could be followed by horrendous ones. This was no exception. Getting to our very own fjord the next day was a brutal journey, starting with a major climb out of Rafsbotn. Then we had to cross the Sennalandet, a barren, exposed piece of tundra usually reserved for cross-country skiing. It was two marathons plus five miles long, all on weary legs. The narrow road had plenty of traffic, rising and falling between sea level and an altitude of 1,000 feet. And lastly, it was bitterly cold – below freezing with the windchill – and the headwind was simply horrendous. Garbage bags that I had managed to scrounge from an aid station were the only things that kept me from hypothermia, once I'd put them on over my Goretex® jacket. I looked such a sight that passengers in several camper vans headed towards us took my photo. These were thirteen more hours I immediately put in the "not fun" column, despite scenery that would've been superb on a sunny day. At least the ending was great; a salmon dinner was on hand as we finished and with only two stages left, optimism was high.

The penultimate stage was another atrocious one; we suffered through gale force headwinds and rain for most of the day and even colder temperatures than we'd encountered previously. Despite wearing tons of layers, the cold just bit through everything I was wearing and then found no body fat resistance. Some aid stations kindly let us warm ourselves for a while inside their vehicles, but that made it even harder to return to the Arctic.

Most of the day was spent moving from fjord to fjord. They were each very beautiful but equally desolate and, absent sunshine, took on a depressing air. We also had to navigate three very dark tunnels, the longest of which was five miles long. It was a spooky feeling – but at least a break from the wind and rain. Arriving in Honningsvåg with only 28 miles left in the race felt delicious. The next day's weather forecast called for more of the same wretched conditions, but we just no longer cared; the end was in sight.

The final day's journey to the finish of the race at the North Cape was desperately difficult. Temperatures hovered just north of freezing, but the constant blasts of icy winds blowing towards us from the polar ice cap – mixed as they were with rain, sleet, hail and snow – made it seem many degrees colder. Sometimes the headwind was so strong that running into it was impossible. I wore two Goretex® jackets, a sweatshirt, and two other shirts, long pants and natty homemade legwarmers, and I swear I never broke a sweat. It was unbelievably, ski-chairlift cold; one guy got frostbite on his nose and I suffered a touch of frostbite on both ear lobes. I have never experienced such bitter gales.

But the race – along with our suffering – was blissfully at an end now we'd reached the northernmost point in Europe. I felt a little "dazed and confused," but I was also inwardly ecstatic at the prospect of not having to tenderize my long-suffering feet again the next day.

Final results
Rainer Koch of Germany dominated and was overall winner, leading Takasumi Senoo (Japan) and René Strosny (Germany) who battled for many days and amazingly finished within less than six minutes of each other. Rainer averaged a mind-blowing 3 hours 30 minutes for each of the 110 marathons he ran during the race.

After Hiroko Okiyama's unfortunate abandon, the women's race was won by another Japanese, Takako Furuyama (20th overall). Second place Elke Streicher of Germany was nearly seven hours behind.

I spent 602 hours crossing Europe and finished 30th out of 67 starters, which pleased me given my advanced years and the quality of the field. Cautious pacing helped me avoid injury. One competition that I <u>did</u> win was body fat loss. According to the

MRI doctors, I finished the race officially devoid of all but a trace of body fat.

When everyone had crossed the finish line, we were bussed back to Honningsvåg. Abba was blasting on the bus' sound system and life was good! When we got back to our sleeping quarters, we threw out all the detritus from nine weeks on the road that we would no longer need, including all those pairs of restyled shoes and socks. After a quick shower, we walked half a mile to the grandest hotel Honningsvåg had to offer for our awards ceremony and final meal together. We quickly dispersed after eating, in order to grab a few short hours of sleep before boarding the Alta airport bus the next morning at 3 a.m.

From the time I woke up the next day, I just couldn't stop eating or thinking about food. My brain and body had suddenly gone into ravenous overdrive. Spending all day on planes or hanging about in Norwegian airports (Alta, Tromsö and Oslo) would cause my credit card to be hit with the equivalent of the GDP of a third world country. How could they justify charging $10 for a shrimp baguette and more than $40 for a pizza?

We set off for Alta airport at 3 a.m. and covered two stages of the race (in the opposite direction, of course) in under two hours. Thanks to it being midsummer, I hadn't seen nighttime darkness in weeks. It didn't really feel like it was that early in the morning (or any other time of day, come to think). I didn't feel so bad, just weary, disconnected and spacey. My packed lunch was gone by 4 a.m. – another record. We crossed the bleak Sennalandet again in wind and pouring rain and saw reindeer by the thousand.

Alta airport was an interesting place in which to reflect at seven o'clock that morning. It's a throwback airport to earlier times when fewer people flew. There were only two check-in desks, courteous ground staff with horrendous, hacking coughs and a snack bar with overpriced coffee and Danish pastries. Much had happened in the last nine weeks. I had crossed six countries on foot. I'd slept on floors, in tents, once in a church and twice in hotel beds. I'd eaten a huge amount by normal standards, a tolerable but monotonous diet high on calories but low on balance and flavor. I'd experienced every form of weather – sun, rain, hail, snow, wind, gales. It had been an extraordinarily arduous journey. I would not have missed it for the world, but I solemnly promised on my blog that I would never do anything so crazy ever again.

I stopped off in the UK to see family on my way home to Texas. On the flight I noticed that my ankles were starting to do an impersonation of water balloons, and my calves, shins and ankles had once again merged to form "cankles" (see Transe Gaule 2005). By the time I landed in Heathrow, my socks had become as tight as sausage skins and the pressure grew more and more painful. It was a little tricky driving my stick shift rental car and trying to take off my socks simultaneously. I was certainly glad that I didn't have to run for a while.

Claire threw me a great party to celebrate my return to Austin, dramatically overcatering with huge quantities of Texas BBQ and Mexican food, margaritas, the works. It was great to have so many friends stop by. Lots of folks said they had enjoyed getting their daily dose of my blog – I let them know that it provided me with an invaluable way to reflect and connect to home. I was just so relieved that the story had a happy ending and could be beautifully recounted in the Austin American-Statesman by my friend Pam LeBlanc.

Now, about that next race...

COOL DOWN

A DAY IN THE LIFE

"Waking up again/To the same old thing/To the same old songs/To the same old pain..."
- Welsh rock band, the Manic Street Preachers

It is 4 a.m. I am lying on a thin air mattress on the floor of a school gymnasium. The air is warm and fetid, as a hundred souls have been sleeping in the same crowded, poorly ventilated space all night. Because it is June and we are north of the Arctic Circle, it is has been light all night outside, but the gym is dimly lit by emergency lights. Every inch of floor space is packed with luggage, bedding and people. Drying clothes and towels hang from every climbing frame and soccer goal net. Last night, each person had constructed a temporary nest in which to bed down for the night, surrounded by their suitcases, running shoes, clothes, food, garbage bags and empty bottles. In the next two hours, any evidence that we ever occupied this space will be gone.

A few people are starting to stir awake. The dawn chorus of hacking coughs, farts and deep exhalations has begun. The earliest risers start to head for the one or two toilets, which are always in desperately short supply. They rise stiffly from their beds, wobbly on tired legs and sore feet. One by one, they shuffle towards a door, which always seems to make undue noise both opening and closing. Another group is starting to awaken, disturbed by the sounds of the already conscious folks, and from within their sleeping bag nest they lie unmoving, starting to prepare mentally for another morning on the road. The rest are still fast asleep, wearing eyeshades and earplugs to maintain a pretense of nighttime.

Wristwatch alarms start to sound, as each individual has calculated how far beyond the prescribed waking time of 4 a.m. they dare to extend their rest. Mine goes off at 4:10 a.m., but I'm always awake earlier. At 4:15 a.m., the overhead lights are turned on, and blinking, exhausted faces look around at each other without any words being exchanged. One alarm clock always sounds last, at 4:20 a.m. It is a hauntingly sweet, gentle tune, but ironically belongs to perhaps the toughest competitor in the race.

The traffic to the bathrooms increases. I have missed the opportunity to hit the toilets early, so I begin the rest of my morning ritual. My sleeping bag is stuffed into its compression sack. I deflate and roll my mattress and tuck eyeshades inside my pillowcase. Then all this bedding is snugly arranged in my suitcase, surrounded by loads of smaller items - computer, flashlight, batteries, laundry soap, vitamins and supplements. I'm already wearing my running shorts for today's stage, so I search for a passably clean shirt or two from the duffle bag containing all my clothes and footwear. Yesterday's shoes and socks worked well, so they'll get reused, but I won't put them on until the very last minute, as my feet are so sore. A pair of crocs™ will suffice until just before the race starts at 6 a.m.

It is still only 4:30 a.m. and breakfast won't begin for at least another twenty minutes, so I optimistically head towards the bathrooms. On the way, I collect a paper cup labeled with my race number – #8 – from a table. This is for my morning urine specimen. Miraculously, a toilet cubicle door is ajar. It smells bad from overuse already this morning, but it's unoccupied, and that's all that matters. On the way back to my nest, I place my half-full #8 cup back on the table, smiling wanly to the impatient line which has formed outside the cubicle door.

Foto: Helmut Dietz

I sit in the folding chair I've wisely brought from home and get out my PDA to check for emails and blog comments. This is a very special time of each day, when I feel like I'm connecting with home, friends and family. I spend ten minutes far away from the activity and commotion of the gym.

Breakfast is theoretically served at 5 a.m., but sometimes it starts a few minutes earlier, so some of us – usually Swedes, Japanese, Germans and I – get lined up early in the hope of getting fed sooner. I never saw French, Dutch or Norwegians in the "early line." There must be something cultural there. The downside of trying to get a jump on breakfast is the risk of upsetting the stern race director's wife, who rules the breakfast and dinner buffets with an iron fist. Sometimes she leniently allows us to sneak in a few minutes early. At other times, she becomes irate, berates us in angry German and throws us out. But hunger makes you take crazy risks like that sometimes.

Once breakfast is dispensed with, we usually have half an hour to prepare for the day's stage. Any final "hygiene" activities get taken care of, as well as last minute packing of toothbrush and warm-up clothes. This is when I finally, reluctantly, put on socks and running shoes which I have delayed thus far to try to avoid as many minutes of unnecessary discomfort as possible.

I usually find myself with a few minutes to spare, so I hand off my two suitcases at the baggage truck and then lie on the gym floor with my feet raised. Many of us do this, side by side. Elevating the feet seems to help reduce swelling and lets gravity send fluid back up the body to where it belongs. Lying down is also another way to minimize effort before the hard work of the day begins.

I check my watch every couple of minutes. Interestingly, those slowest at preparing for the day ahead are also the slowest runners. With only five minutes to go until the 6 a.m. start, I often observe two Japanese ladies who will finish in the last two positions overall still putting lotion on their feet, surrounded by their unpacked luggage and belongings. How they ever made it to the finish still mystifies me.

Finally, race director Ingo walks through the gym announcing the imminent start. We slowly make our way outside – very slowly if it is raining – and stand mute while the Japanese take photos of each other under the start banner. And they do this not once or twice during the race, but every day for 64 days. Remarkable.

"Ready for start?" Ingo gravely and rhetorically intones. As the weeks pass, initial exuberance has turned to glum acceptance of what lays ahead. Ingo begins to countdown from ten – the keenest joining in loudly in their native language, the rest mumbling along in faltering English. Others check watches, make wisecracks or re-lace shoes. On the command "Go!" muffled cheers from the twenty or so spectators on hand send us on our way to begin another stage. Some run right from the start, others trot along at a very slow clip, and the rest walk the first mile or so to get muscles and joints back to the business of running again. Every morning it seems to me that there has been so little time since we'd stopped running the previous evening that my legs and feet haven't had any real chance to recover.

It is fortunately daylight at the start (and has been since the first three weeks of the race). Having to run the first hour or so in the dark is always a much more dispiriting beginning of the day for me. Even so, the wonderful sunrises which we had witnessed from time to time in Italy and Germany were a reenergizing, distracting way to start the day.

The first few miles of each stage pass slowly. I feel as if I am running in slow motion. I look around to see who's feeling good today and who's suffering. It's easy to tell. Anyone feeling good is already in front of me, running smoothly and moving away from me. The sufferers are lagging behind – sometimes way behind – trying to get sore muscles or aching joints working again.

As we leave our overnight town, we quickly reach open countryside. Because of the earliness of the hour, we only occasionally see a car or pedestrian heading to work. We're always gone well ahead of what passes for the "rush hour" this far north.

The first hour is spent remembering how to run and expending as little energy as possible in the process. Once into the second hour, thoughts turn to the first aid station, which is usually operated by Ramona, the race masseuse and, since last year, the wife of one of the German runners Joachim Hauser. I always look forward to visiting with Ramona. I like her attitude and her love of Joachim, who's dealing with significant health issues. I get a big daily dose of positive energy from Ramona, plus two cups of apple juice.

By the time two hours are completed, I've finished my "second breakfast" – a ham and cheese roll – which I'd sneaked from the breakfast buffet three hours ago, and I'm looking forward to aid station number two. Two German ladies – spouses of other race staff – are in charge of this one. They are a joy too and always very solicitous about my welfare. As they see me in the distance coming towards them, they grab a chair for me to sit on. By now they've learned my preference for seated repose. We exchange pleasantries, I commiserate with them about the usually abysmal weather they have to stand around in, I eat and drink as much as I can face and then it's up again, and back to work.

The pattern repeats at each of the next six aid stations. The only exception is at aid station number five, which is manned by Tomas, his wife and their young son Samuel. They miraculously manage to produce hot soup for us each day, usually mixed with leftovers from last night's dinner. Tomas lights a campfire by his campervan, and sometimes the smoke can be seen for quite a time before reaching them. It is a wonderful sight to behold – it signifies that the day's effort is about two-thirds done.

The final aid station of the day is managed by Uli, a preacher from Dresden. His signature mark is a chalk inscription on the road about one kilometer before his station. Seeing this sign always gives a hugely welcome sense of being "nearly done" with another day. Uli is another great character, overflowing with kindness and empathy. He often tries to shop for local delicacies for us before we arrive. Occasionally I try some new, tasty treat which Uli has conjured up from somewhere, but I usually regret it later. Spicy sausages, fish paste or fatty slices of ham aren't digestively the best things to try for the first time mid-race.

Uli lets us know how many kilometers there are to the finish, anywhere between seven and twelve usually. That means at least one more hour of running. Those final kilometers always seem interminable, but closing in on another finish is still a joy. There are just two burning questions on everyone's minds that we pose to Uli: How big is the gym we're staying in? And are the showers hot?

We'll soon find out. Chalk arrows on the ground direct us to the finish line for the stage. Often we'll see some of the speedier runners who've already showered and changed roaming the streets in search of food, drink and other supplies. They cheer us on and lift our spirits. We finally pass under the finish banner and make sure the timekeeper has recorded our time for the day.

We head into the gym and start to search for our

baggage, looking all the while for any free, comfortable place to sleep. Once everything's been located and laid out on the best piece of floor available, it's time to eat, shower and then rest before dinner. Most people wear their sweaty running clothes into the shower, and wash them before taking them off. Thank heaven for modern, quick drying fabrics. I notice that the length of time spent washing our bodies is directly proportional to the warmth of the water.

If the day's stage has been "short" – in other words, less than ten hours' running – then there's usually an opportunity for some sleeping bag time. After rest or sleep comes dinner, usually at 7 p.m. If we're lucky, it's served in the gym itself. If not, a walk to a nearby restaurant may be required; even walking a quarter of a mile is resented as unnecessary time spent on tired legs. We eat whatever is served. There's no choice, but no-one complains. We're all ravenous. The meal is usually finished in thirty minutes flat.

Here's an unscientific but remarkably instructive pie chart showing how each day is spent. Notice how small one particular slice – **FUN!** – is:

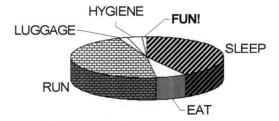

And so to bed. Another day done and checked off.

What will tomorrow be like? It's likely to be pretty much the same. Just remember the Bill Murray movie, "Groundhog Day".

"Finish each day and be done with it. You have done what you could. Some blunders and absurdities no doubt crept in, forget them as soon as you can. Tomorrow is a new day, you shall begin it well and serenely..."
- Ralph Waldo Emerson

INTERESTING CHARACTERS

"Insane people are always sure that they are fine. It is only the sane people who are willing to admit that they are crazy."
- Nora Ephron

I enjoyed getting to know some of my fellow transcontinental runners – the "normal", the eccentric and the decidedly odd. I'll concede that it does take an unusual kind of person to attempt to run across a continent. Different runners certainly had different motivations and goals for the race, which transcended age, gender and national background. I got to know many of them quite well over the course of nine weeks, and I gradually developed an informal taxonomy for the ultrarunning genus.

Some runners were balanced, easy-going, thoughtful individuals on a mission to complete the journey to the North Cape; I'll call them "normal people" and will immodestly put myself in that category. Normal is a relative word, of course, but I use the term here to describe people with average social skills, a thoughtful outlook on life, the ability to share, "play nice" and demonstrate consideration for others.

Members of the next group were out to win; let's call them the "the competitors." There were at least ten superb athletes who pushed very hard throughout the race to finish high up in the rankings. In the end, Rainer Koch dominated this category on the men's side of the race. Hiroko Okiyama would have done likewise for the women if bad injuries hadn't sidelined her very close to the finish. Both these individuals, I should quickly add, are also "normal" according to my definition above.

The third group I put into a "running fanatic" category, meaning that running dominated their thoughts, interests and conversation. It appeared that all they did in life was to run as many marathons and ultras as possible. They could reel off endless statistics about their training mileage, racing performances and next-up races. I knew I did not belong in this category, as I've never kept a running log, can't remember my times and during Trans Europe had no intention of ever running that far again, if I were to reach the finish.

The final group I'll dub "plain crazy". One way these runners could be distinguished from other members of the group was by talking to themselves in the gym at night while showing only a passing interest in others around them. Even after being forced to abandon the race due to injury, they would insist on continuing to run many stages – or parts of stages – instead of doing the logical thing – going home to rest and recover.

At the risk of "kissing and telling," I've included some thoughts on a few of the different personalities who added color to the Trans Europe party:

GPS Man

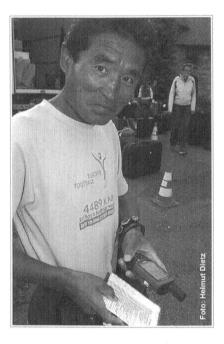

One competitor ran carrying a hand-held GPS device in his left hand, wore a watch on his left wrist and held route directions in his right hand. As soon as the start command was issued each morning, he began a kind of obsessive-compulsive ritual of checking GPS, watch and route directions *at least every fifty meters*. It was particularly bizarre and redundant when we reached Scandinavia, because for days on end we followed the same road all day. What information was being imparted to him was always a mystery to me. Because his English was as poor as my Japanese, I was never able to ask him what on earth he needed to check and why he needed to check that data so frequently.

In the first weeks of the race, I had run wearing a Garmin® GPS. I found it quite useful and reassuring to know how far I'd traveled through each stage and how far I still had to go. But by the time we'd reached Northern Germany, I'd managed to destroy it by dropping it on a tiled shower floor. Mild panic set in, and I even asked Claire to send me a replacement, but I soon found that I didn't really need its help. After four weeks, my brain it seemed had developed a metronomic sense of steady pace and so I no longer needed to rely on electronic gadgetry.

Marmalade crazies

The one thing guaranteed to create uproar and mayhem amongst the German speakers at the breakfast buffet line was absence of jam (*Marmalade*, in German). It made grown men frantic and inconsolable until some could finally be produced. I heard it stated with furious passion more than once that it is impossible to eat breakfast without jam.

Coughing Man

About ten days into the race, one of the Japanese competitors developed a horrendous, hacking cough. At first, this was not unusual, as lots of folks – runners and volunteers alike – became quite sick with colds and coughs around this time. But Coughing Man took his coughing to a new level. It was almost performance art. If we'd been in a tuberculosis ward, he would have fit right in. He coughed morning, noon and night. All night, sometimes. And loudly. The race doctors finally checked him with a stethoscope and pronounced him fit enough to continue. There was an implication that his problem was psychosomatic, as he apparently always coughed like that at home. Well, let me tell you, after my initial sympathy had worn thin, he made me – and many other runners – nail-spittingly mad. Mad on two levels – he was disturbing everyone's precious rest, but worse than that, he was potentially infecting us all with some god-awful chest infection which could have wrecked our chances of making it to Norway.

After about three weeks, he was sent into a form of quarantine by his fellow Japanese runners. Even they – long-suffering as they were – had had enough of him. Each night, he was made to bed down in a shower room, broom closet or some other isolated place. Once in a while I felt a tinge of sympathy for him but at the same time wanted to personally put him on the next plane home to Tokyo. Finally, he was forced to abandon and spend a day at a hospital in Sweden, getting checked out. That night, he was back with us, coughing as usual, with an apparently clean bill of health, and he continued to run the rest of the race to the North Cape as a stage runner.

The #34 Shuffle

Many runners – especially the Japanese men in the race – had a shuffling style of distance running. Nothing wrong with that, you think. Well, no, not for the first hour or two. But after that, it becomes irritating, then annoying, then really, desperately, mind-blowingly maddening. "Pick up your feet!" you scream inside your head. "Don't you realize that it's inefficient to scuff along like that?!" The very worst offender was competitor #34, and it was in his honor that we christened this insufferable behavior the #34 Shuffle.

German ladies

Four German ladies competed in the race. They didn't seem to care for each other. Nor for the most part did they seem to give a hoot about the rest of the group – runners, volunteers or race organizers – judging from their almost pathological aversion to politeness. A couple of them created more issues for the race director than everyone else combined, showing a constant narcissistic desire for acceptance, but giving out nothing in return except negative energy. Maybe it was a cultural thing, but not many of the German speakers appeared to relate particularly well to them either.

The Princess

Once done with running each day, one of the female competitors always appeared to be in everyone else's business, constantly "cruise directing" her countrymen and women. When not doing that, she made an art form of giving the race organizers a really hard time about things that were not within their control. Another source of negative energy, when what you really need is great teamwork and support.

The Swedish Army

Two Swedish soldiers ran the whole race together, almost in lockstep, even during a particularly tough week when one of them was suffering from a serious leg injury. Despite the stress and physical hardship, they never wavered in their support of the race organizers, other runners or each other. They lightened the mood when needed and provided a great linguistic bridge between different cultures and nationalities, becoming a vital ingredient in the race's social dynamic and logistics.

Their English was wonderful, naturally, and so it was a great pleasure eating dinner with them, which we did together many times. I thoroughly enjoyed their company, courtesy, helpfulness and brilliant sense of humor.

Foto: Helmut Dietz

NERDY DATA

I did some interesting graphing things with Excel, and took a look at my performance over the course of my three big races. I plotted both daily and average cumulative speed.

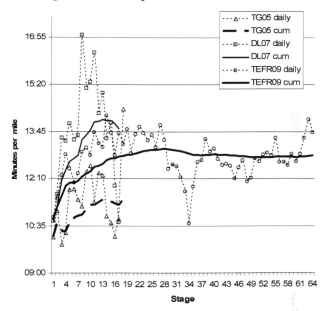

Some observations I was able to glean from all these curves and datapoints:

o   My best performance of the three races was clearly **Transe Gaule** 2005 (TG05). The outlying datapoint on the last day of the race was due to our wait before the finish so that we could cross the line together as a group. I was at my youngest in 2005 – a callow 50 years of age – and my legs had many less miles on them then.

Days with slower speeds correlate directly to days injured during this race.

o I performed at my abject worst at **Deutschlandlauf** in 2007 (DL07), even though the race included far fewer days than Trans Europe (TEFR09). I ascribe this in large part to the injury problems I had to deal with before and during that race, in addition to the very hard, long early stages.

o The plateauing of my **Trans Europe** performance occurred around Stage 28, as we arrived in Scandinavia. Germany was relatively hilly, and so my slow decrease in speed was in large part due to that.

o A revealing part of the curves is my obvious tendency to go more quickly in the first few days of each race and then slow down significantly. Apart from rank stupidity on my part, this is also a result of cumulative fatigue which always builds during the first ten days or so of each race.

o There is a lot of variability in daily performance when compared to the trend of cumulative performance. The biggest factors affecting daily speed are the length and relative hilliness of the stage, the impact of weather (especially headwinds and high temperatures) and the effects of any injuries.

WHY? AND HOW?

THE BIG QUESTION

"All men should strive to learn before they die, what they are running from, and to, and why."
- James Thurber, American author, cartoonist and celebrated wit

In the tiny town of Lit in Sweden, I had just finished running for 10 hours. Stage 45 of the Trans Europe Footrace 2009 was done and 19 stages still remained. Athletes, volunteers, medics and race director had been on the road for over six weeks and the fatigue and stress from the journey thus far was palpable. I was sitting weary and doleful in Lit's school gym, our sleeping quarters for the night, eying my heap of belongings and trying to get motivated to take a shower. It was part of the daily end-of-stage ritual. First, find your bags and locate mattress, sleeping bag and pillow. Place them strategically in the best possible remaining, unclaimed spot on the gym floor, to avoid getting stepped on at night by somnambulists heading to the bathroom. Next, dig through your luggage to find a passably clean change of clothes, towel and washing stuff. Hobble to the shower; wash your filthy running clothes and yourself and then try to nap briefly before dinner.

But on this day, a teenaged student named Richard approached me, explaining that his class was studying English. He asked if I would come and speak to them about America and the Footrace. Truth be told, I groaned inwardly – all I really wanted to do was lie down and rest – but I did relish the idea of meeting young Swedes in their native habitat. So I agreed, following Richard out of the gym and across the school playground. It was windy, freezing, and rain was falling. Richard was wearing a T-shirt and barely seemed to notice the atrocious weather. To him, this was summer. I was bundled up yet still bitterly cold.

I was ushered into his classroom of perhaps twenty students and a very cool teacher. I had become today's "show and tell" exhibit, as I proceeded to describe Texas, its weather and its geography to them. I was able to ask some questions back – "Do you like living in Sweden?" Unequivocally yes! "Do you like the weather here?" Yes indeed, seven months of snow each year is great! "Don't the winter months get depressing with so little daylight?" Hmmm, they hadn't really thought about that...

Then we got to talk about the Trans Europe Footrace. I pointed out the route on a map of Europe and talked a little about the course so far – the Adriatic coast of Italy, the Po Valley, the Austrian Alps, Bavaria, the rest of Germany, and southern Sweden. After a few practical questions from the kids, the teacher stepped in and posed me the hardest but simplest question of all – "Why?"

There was a long pause while I tried to get my thoughts together. He'd really asked the tough one. Why do apparently rational adults take on something as difficult, and at times as dangerous, as running across a continent? I rambled on about the challenge and about meeting new people, but it was a simple question to which I didn't really provide a very cogent response. That teacher's question stayed with me for many days on the road, when I would have abundant time to reflect.

Throughout the ages, runners have been quizzed about their motivations for their apparently bizarre impulse to expend what sedentary folk see as unnecessary effort. For example, in Dean Karnazes' book, *Ultramarathon Man*, Dean tries to answer these "simple" questions about himself: What am I running from? Who am I running for? And where am I running to?

Dean had an epiphany on his thirtieth birthday, when he figured out that working too hard and playing too hard were unhealthy lifestyle choices. He started running that night, went on to run longer and longer distances, and eventually became the public relations face of ultrarunning in the US. In the final analysis, Dean points out that he likes the solitude of running; he believes it allows him to enjoy and inspire people around him more; and he runs in part because he's "not much of a car guy."

I can't claim any such pivotal moment in my life, but Dean's analysis resonates well with me. I've always run, whether to stay in shape, to compete in races, or just to exercise my dogs. I like to run alone, even though I enjoy the company of my fellow runners…up to a point![26] I don't like sitting in cars much, and nothing makes me happier than when I inspire even just one person to get off the couch and get healthier.

I think I've made a difference to two of the people closest to me. While I was on my transcontinental adventure, my daughter Tracey who lives in England with her husband and two young babies

---

[26] To quote runner and author Haruki Murakami: "I'm the type of person who *doesn't find it painful* to be alone."

emailed me with fantastic news. My run had helped inspire her to enter her very first 10K. I was ecstatic for her when she pushed herself to achieve that goal. It cast my mind back fondly 25 years, as I reminisced about my wife's – her mother's – first 10K, which we ran together in a New Jersey race. Claire has since gone on to be an excellent athlete in her own right, running the Boston Marathon multiple times, completing an Ironman and representing Team USA at the Triathlon World Championships.

But the question still remains – why are some people so driven and others not? Why did I take on these challenges in my fifties? For me, I will put it down to my pre-teen and teen years' education.

I grew up in England, and up until the age of twelve attended a small private school. We had a fierce, sadistic head teacher, Mr. Lewis, who terrified me and all my fellow students. He was so scary he could make kids lose bladder control. One aspect of his neo-Dickensian approach was to make us run around the perimeter of the local park twice a week, during the period euphemistically entitled "Games." He particularly favored those bitter English afternoons when the ground was frozen too hard for soccer. We were allowed nothing like sweatshirts or gloves to help improve the experience. And Mr. Lewis certainly did not allow walking. Back then, people thought corporal punishment was a pretty reasonable way to treat little kids, and so he beat children he saw dallying with a tennis shoe. I'm here to tell you that a mix of pain and public humiliation is a great athletic motivator. It took me several decades before I could comfortably take a walk break during a workout.

On the positive side, I thrived academically at that school. The pressure was intense[27], but every ounce of potential was extracted from each student. At each years' prize giving ceremony, I won various prizes and commendations. But there was one award that I coveted more than anything else and never won. It took the form of a small lapel pin with the word **PERSEVERANCE** written across it. The winner of that award got to wear the pin for the entire year that followed. How I coveted that award – I was green with envy at the lucky classmate who got to wear it. Looking back, I realize that the perseverance prize was given to kids who were less academically able but who nonetheless tried hard. I had no chance of ever winning that award, being both smart and lazy. But the result, as I entered my teens, was a lurking self-doubt that I was not the persevering type. I still had something to prove to Mr. Lewis, my parents and the world.

In my early teens, I joined a rowing club. The adult members of the club needed kids to steer their racing boats, and because I was willing to do this was warmly welcomed into their midst. What I observed at first shocked me – but also impressed me enormously. Grown men would row a dozen "intervals" up and down a 500-meter straightaway as hard as they could. They would frequently get to the end and then proceed to vomit over the side of the boat, so hard had they pushed themselves. After a while, and once I became big and strong enough to row with them, I came to see this behavior as normal. It was an understood part of the physical sacrifice needed to excel and win races.

---

[27] I started learning Latin at age seven, for example.

Meanwhile, I had moved on to a "rugby school" for my high school years. Schools in England are still divided into "rugby" or "football" (i.e., soccer) schools, depending on their history and past victories. I took my rowing experience – and all its masochistic hours of self-discipline and self-sacrifice – directly onto the rugby field, where I worked my sorry butt off to cover as much of the field as I could during every workout and every game. I was a fierce, aggressive competitor back then – so much so that my mother couldn't stand to watch me play. What I lacked in skill, I made up for in drive, determination, physical conditioning and recklessness.

I also enjoyed some success at middle distance track and cross-country running, but those were always seen as "minor" sports back then. I had a very strong kick and couldn't stand to be beaten. With coaching, I could've been more successful, I think, but team sports were the thing back then. Football in Texas dominates high school sports programs in much the same way today.

So now fast forward to the "grown man" at Trans Europe. Gone is the aggressive and bruising competitor; the passage of time and lower levels of testosterone probably took care of that. But there's still something to prove – a dread of failure, of stopping, of giving up.

Maybe if they'd given me that damned **PERSEVERANCE** lapel pin all those years ago, I would never have gotten to write this story.

GETTING IT DONE

"…we don't have a lot of time on this earth. Human beings weren't meant to sit in little cubicles, staring at computer screens all day, filling out useless forms and listening to eight different bosses drone on about mission statements."
- Peter Gibbons (Ron Livingston) in the movie "Office Space"

One thing's for sure – ultra stage races are nothing like big city marathons. There is little glamour or glitz associated with these races. They are intense but extensive; races are complex but at the same time very low-key experiences for competitors, volunteers and race staff alike. Although technically called "races", they become so much more – a short-term way of life for those involved. They're timed in weeks rather than hours and minutes, and end up a defining personal experience and journey for most. Every runner is competing against fatigue and injury, which become constant, unwelcome companions, more than against his or her fellow athletes.

These races are brutally demanding events. It is essential to plan, prepare and execute well in order to have any chance of getting past the first few days of the race. Luck also plays a huge hand in the outcome. Like poker, it's not always the person with the best hand – or even a good hand – that wins.

Planning

"Always have a plan, and believe in it. Nothing happens by accident."
- Chuck Knox, former NFL head coach

Plans need both short- and long-term components. It's not possible to complete a major stage race on a whim. In my case, I spent the best part of seven years getting to be a transcontinental runner, taking on longer and harder races every two years. I didn't plan this all in one go, but rather had a "rolling" two year plan that evolved. At any given time, though, I always had one big race that I was working towards mapped out in the future – sometimes as far as eighteen months away – to keep me motivated and focused each day and every workout.

Preparation

"Plans are only good intentions unless they immediately degenerate into hard work."
- Peter Drucker, management consultant and writer

Fortunately, running is not a difficult or technically challenging thing to do. Billions of human beings learn to do it successfully as children. We are not taught to run; it is a skill innate in almost everyone on the planet. However, running distances greater than the human body is designed to cover in one effort (somewhere around fifteen miles) does require significant amounts of conditioning and training. Repeating that feat for many days in a row requires even more preparation.

There are three components of my training. The first is mileage, all of which is now done at slow, comfortable pace. A "long" week for me is more than 100 miles; a "short" week is less than fifty. I rotate through short, medium and long weeks every three weeks in order to keep fresh in the six months leading up to each big race. The next important component is what I call back-to-back days – runs of thirteen miles or more on three or more consecutive days. These efforts condition the body to repair quickly and deal with the minimal recovery periods you get during a stage race. The last component is "two-a-days" – days when I run long twice. My commute to work was twelve miles long, so I would often run to work in the morning and home again that evening for a two-a-day workout totaling 24 miles leading up to each of my big events.

All of this requires significant commitment, but I'm pretty flexible in my preparation. If I have to miss a workout because of, say, a business trip, I don't fixate; I just adjust my schedule after the fact. It's important for me to take a long, laid back view on things. That doesn't mean that I'm a slacker – I actually do put in a lot of effort and run a lot of miles to get ready, but total training done is all that really matters. I never fret about one individual missed workout.

In addition to running lots of miles, I do two other things to condition my body and avoid injury. Once or twice a week I go to the gym for a "spin class" – stationary biking seems to help my cardiovascular system and increases leg strength without additional pavement pounding. I also spend half an hour each evening lying on my bedroom floor (watching a TV show to mitigate the boredom) doing exercises to strengthen my core muscle groups, mixed in with some gentle stretching. I never lift big weights or swim, and these days I severely limit time spent trail running, just because I don't want to run the risk of injury.

Throughout the preparation phase, I try to eat a

good diet, get plenty of rest and stay healthy. I generally eat OK, but I'm a poor, very light sleeper. Fortunately, I manage to remain very healthy despite – or because of? – the load I place on my body.

Execution

"The fundamental qualities for good execution of a plan is first; intelligence; then discernment and judgment, which enable one to recognize the best method as to attain it; the singleness of purpose; and, lastly, what is most essential of all, will - stubborn will."
- Marshal Ferdinand Foch, French general during World War I

Want to know my stage race strategy? That's easy:
> Start very slowly.
> Eat and drink lots at every aid station.
> Waste no unnecessary energy.
> Walk up any real incline.
> Never give up, and just get it done.

That's it. That's my strategy.

I don't listen to music while I run, mainly because of traffic; I like to hear what's going on around me in case I ever need to take evasive action. I tend to run alone for two reasons – to avoid running either too fast or too slow, and because it makes me uncomfortable running two abreast when there are cars and trucks whizzing by. I'm quite happy with my own company and do a lot of thinking during those long hours out there on the route. Deep down, the feeling of getting it done pleases and satisfies me.

The most important thing that I keep focused on at

all times is what people refer to as "Eyes on the Prize." Unless you stand a chance of finishing top three on the podium, the only objective I worry about at any point in a stage race is actually finishing. As Stefan Schlett, a Trans America 1992 finisher, observed to me earlier this year, no-one cares when you get home which place you finished. People only want to know that you made it. So that's "the Prize" – it's that simple. If you are well prepared, all that finishing requires is intelligent pacing, common sense, support from the race organization, stubborn will, and luck. Nothing more nor less.

Attitude

"Nothing can stop the man with the right mental attitude from achieving his goal; nothing on earth can help the man with the wrong mental attitude."
- Thomas Jefferson, the third US president

People often – only half-jokingly – ask whether I and my fellow ultra runners are crazy. As with any group of people, generalizing is a dangerous thing to do. On top of that, craziness is a very hard thing to define. For some outsiders, the desire to want to run megamiles defines crazy. For others, crazy starts somewhere north of five miles. Others still see the marathon as the "crazy watershed."

I will say from personal experience that while some of my fellow ultra stage runners are very eccentric and odd, most are perfectly rational and sane. As I've spent time getting to know them – and myself – I've observed a certain set of key personality traits which I believe help to dramatically improve the odds of finishing.

First and foremost is what I'll call **realistic self-confidence**. Deep down inside, ultra stage runners need to believe that they can prevail and make it to the finish line – in other words, they need to possess what might be seen as **inner strength**. They have to see things from a **positive perspective** at all times – the glass must always be "half full" – whatever the race, the weather or the terrain throws at them.

Next, they need a Zen-like attitude – they must on the one hand be enormously **focused** but on the other remain **balanced**. These races can't be undertaken lightly, but folks who take them too seriously often end up quitting ahead of those who just see them as adventures.

Almost self evidently, ultra runners must be **risk-takers**. Most races are journeys into uncharted territory which the risk averse wouldn't even want to try. Along with that attitude must come **adaptability** and **problem solving.** Over so many days and miles, things can – and certainly will – go horribly wrong at times. The ability to adapt and accept those minor or even major disasters is what stops people from abandoning.

Lastly, I think ultra runners benefit from a great **sense of humor**. You can certainly get by without one, but when the chips are down and everything is in the crapper, so to speak, laughter is a great antidote. Aid station volunteers are particularly drawn to happy, upbeat and positive runners, and that in turn I believe helps them to provide the very best care they can to you as a runner.

I love this brilliantly well-observed quote on this

subject by Dr. Rowly Brucken from an essay entitled, "Who are we? A paradoxical explanation of Ultrarunning":

"Ultrarunners...have to possess an inner core of arrogance. We think we are supermen and superwomen, that we are mentally and physically tougher than most, and...possess the resources to triumph in the end. And yet ultrarunners are some of the most humble, friendly, approachable people I know. We intimately know our bodies and minds and how vulnerable and frail they can be. We know of failure, of injuries that take too long to heal, of having to drop out of a race. We know of the necessity of teamwork with pacers, supporters, race volunteers, and communion with complete strangers on the course that will get us through the dark miles. Everyone who finishes can give thanks for the love, patience and support of others. We each know this, and we are proud of ourselves and grateful for others...."

Luck

"Zeus does not bring all men's plans to fulfillment."
- Homer, from The Iliad

Luck plays a huge part in successfully completing any ultra stage race. Anyone who thinks or tells you otherwise is dead wrong. You can prepare all you like, you can have the perfect training plan, you can take endless steps to avoid illness and injury, you can eat and sleep right but, at the end of the day, disaster can strike. The longer and further the race, the greater the odds of encountering bad luck.

The single most important piece of luck needed is

wrapped up in one's DNA – having "chosen one's parents wisely" as the saying goes. Without the right lucky accident of birth, this ultra thing could never work. A suitable body type, sound biomechanics and healthy cardiovascular system are just some of the basic building blocks for aspiring ultra runners.

Your parents and upbringing must also have imbued you with the right mental spirit and drive to allow you to want to endure days of hardship and privation before and during the race. Both "nature" and "nurture" play key roles in starting and then eventually finishing a major stage race.

The final huge slice of luck needs to happen immediately before and during the race. So many things can go wrong. Contracting a nasty upper respiratory infection or stepping in a big pothole in the road – these are just two examples of the many hundreds of race-ending tripwires which criss-cross the long journey to the finish line.

NUTRITION

One apparent upside of running all day long is it gives you license to consume all and everything placed in front of you. From waking up in the morning to going to sleep at night, food becomes a constant preoccupation. I'm often asked how many calories I consume per day on a race. I'm not a calorie counter, but my unscientific guess would be somewhere north of 8,000. By the end of stage races, I have usually managed to lose at least ten pounds off my extremely lean frame. As my wife Claire confirms when I get home, it's not a pretty sight.

Going into Trans Europe, I had been trying (too successfully, as it turned out!) to lower my elevated cholesterol. Claire and I had gone on a vegan-type diet, along the lines of the *Engine 2 Diet* recommended by our Austin firefighter and athlete friend, Rip Esselstyn. A year or so back, my doctor had prescribed the statin Lipitor for me, which for me had proved to be an unmitigated disaster. I'd suffered all kinds of muscle aches and other problems with the drug, and quit "cold turkey" after a couple of weeks. This year, though, changing to a largely "plant based" diet had done the trick for me, causing my cholesterol numbers to tumble thirty points in a month.

The downside, however, was that I went into the race with significantly reduced body fat. I had also intended to take the "vegetarian" option at mealtimes during the race. Both these things proved problematic.

With little fat to draw on, my body soon became progressively more depleted, lacking the energy stores needed to help it get through its daily mileage. What I also learned from the medical team is that internal organs are surrounded by fat stores, which help to cushion and protect them from each other. Without fat, the organs rub against or bump into each other and, in extreme cases, internal bleeding can result. So, obviously, while you don't want to carry pounds of unnecessary fat, you still do need a healthy sufficiency.

Some research when I got home confirmed this. Howard Flaks, a Californian who specializes in obesity treatment, had this to say on the Maxim website: "…A certain amount of body fat is essential to cushion the joints, protect the organs and help regulate body temperature, as well as to store vitamins and help the body sustain itself when food is not available. Therefore, it's possible to have a body fat percentage that's too low…I believe some people can go as low as five per cent, but certainly not below that. Some researchers feel that…strength and mental concentration deteriorate below seven per cent body fat. As well, loss of muscle can occur below five per cent, as the body will turn to muscle for fuel in the absence of fat…."

During the race, we were "measured" by the medics every three days – weight, temperature, blood pressure and body fat – and MRI'd once a week. I'm not sure what happened to my mental concentration, but my body fat test results were very low – and always below five percent after the first few days of the race. I struggled to increase my fat intake during the race, and certainly felt that my muscles weakened due to poor diet, particularly in Italy.

Eating a vegetarian diet proved almost impossible. The race organization valiantly tried to provide vegetarian meals early on, but because they were usually at the mercy of local vendors who didn't seem to understand the needs of "veg-heads", they couldn't provide a sufficient diet for the few who'd checked the vegetarian box on the race application form. Within a couple of weeks of the start, I believe that almost every vegetarian runner had by necessity turned omnivore.

Meat became more plentiful once we'd crossed into Austria, and then fish became more common in

Scandinavia. But Southern Italy was where we had the biggest dietary issues. Meals early in the race were very carbohydrate heavy, in the form of copious pasta. This was filling but not sufficiently balanced (for me at least) with protein and fat. A ladle of Bolognese sauce, while delicious, doesn't provide much of either. For non-runners, therefore, it's quite healthy; for us, it became a curse.

To help the situation, I started to supplement the race's provisions with additional things like macadamia nuts (which are high in fat and protein), beef jerky and pickled herring. For additional fat and general digestion, I washed my post-race snacks down with a big tub of yoghurt each day. I tried to eat as soon as possible after finishing each stage, as I've heard that the body processes food intake most efficiently right after exercise.

Breakfasts were usually a typical European amalgam of good stuff – bread, butter, jam, cheese, cold meats, fruit, cereal, coffee, tea and juice. The further north we got, breakfasts became even better with the welcome appearance of both oatmeal and fish. Often, we were rationed to two rolls for breakfast, but there was usually additional bread. My personal favorite turned out to be the chocolate spread Nutella®, which I applied liberally to a couple of thick slices of bread. Whenever there was extra, I would sneak an extra roll with ham and cheese, putting it in my jacket pocket in a plastic bag to act as my "second breakfast" between the start line and the first aid station. I felt this gave me a much needed energy boost.

During the race itself, I made sure to eat and drink at every aid station without fail. At the speed I was running, these came along roughly every ninety minutes. While many runners preferred to stand and eat, I always took the seated option. It seemed to help my back and leg problems, as sitting allowed my tired muscles to relax.

Typically, I would drink two cups of apple juice and eat a ham or salami and cheese sandwich with lots of salt and pickled gherkins, washed down by a piece of fruit (apple or banana) and couple of slices of cake. I then grabbed a couple of handfuls of chocolate chip cookies, which I ate as I left the aid station and started down the road again. I also stuffed two or three candy bars in my pockets; these would tide me over until I reached the next aid station. I had a very bad moment at the end of one long stage when my blood sugar zoomed very low and I had no food with me; after that, I always made sure to keep some licorice candies in a plastic bag in my jacket pocket for such emergencies.

The fourth or fifth aid station each day was always a special one, as hot noodle or rice soup was served there. Reaching this point each day was a great physical and mental boost. Dinner was less predictable, but again once north of Italy usually provided a sufficient amount of good food. My only reservation was that the food was not very spicy or inspiring. I found myself longing for a Szechuan dish or a good Indian curry.

Reading this back, it looks like an exaggeratedly large daily diet. Not so. I really did consistently consume this volume of food each and every day. My only other intake was a bunch of daily supplements in pill form. I always take glucosamine for my joints, which seems to help; despite one knee meniscus surgery, I don't seem to have significant problems there. To avoid shin splints, I take a calcium supplement, as I don't find European diets to be particularly calcium-rich. I take vitamin C, too, and this seems to help mitigate (but not really avoid or eliminate) the effects of the common cold.

SHOES

Everyone asks about shoes – especially the "How many pairs do you get through?" question. Shoes are obviously a very important consideration – in the final analysis, they can make the difference between finishing a race comfortably and having to abandon. Here's what I tell them:

Modern running shoes are generally good for about 500 miles per pair. Some runners trash their shoes in many less miles than that; I can usually make mine last for nearly 1,000 miles but by then they are starting to lose their cushioning and taking on a very stiff feel.

Multiday races are tricky to buy shoes for because a week or so into the race feet can swell by an entire size. For Trans Europe, I took two sets of shoes, abandoning the smaller sized pairs after the first two weeks.

Choice of brand isn't critical to me; these days most of the major manufacturers produce well constructed, high quality shoes. But I will confess to a weakness for New Balance shoes for two reasons: (a) they are the best at offering their styles in wide widths which my feet require, and (b) they kindly gave me half-a-dozen pairs as a form of *quid pro quo* sponsorship for Trans Europe. Thanks to them for that.

What's important in selecting shoes is a great – not just good – fit, the right amount of cushioning, and as little weight as reasonable given the first two requirements. I have very high arches and sensitive heels, so support for those either needs to be provided by the shoe and its insole "out of the box" from the manufacturer, or by adding after-market heat moldable footbed inserts like the ones I bought from *yoursole.com*. These worked very well for me for the most part, although they are slightly heavy and are not quite as cushiony as I would have liked.

One trick that I've always employed since 2007 is to completely remove the toe boxes of my sneakers, right up to the laces (pictured in the Deutschlandlauf chapter). The shoes work perfectly well without them, at least on non-trail surfaces. Doing this helps prevent the friction that causes blisters and lets my feet "breathe". My toes don't get cold and I have never had problems with crud from the road entering the shoe from the front end, although that's often what people assume.

INJURY AND ILLNESS

The first thing to know about ultra stage races is that everyone – and I seriously mean everyone – battles at least one form of injury during each race. No-one is spared, from the fastest to the slowest. Most runners can also expect to get sick at least once on a stage race of any length. Some of these problems can develop into "showstoppers", but what's critical is figuring out early how best to deal with them before they force the runner out of the race completely.

The most common problems runners experience are **common colds and URIs** (upper respiratory infections). Because immune systems are compromised by fatigue and hygiene is poor, colds and coughs seem to pass quickly and freely among participants. Frankly there isn't much that can be done to speed their departure. I find that running actually feels better than sitting around moping – maybe because the release of adrenalin seems to suppress the worst cold symptoms. **Bronchitis** is quite common too and certainly more troubling; it can be caused by both bacteria and viruses, and needs to be watched carefully. Antibiotics will have no effect if the form is viral; drinking extra liquid and taking over the counter remedies are probably the only things that can effectively provide any relief mid-race.

The other common issue runners are likely to face are GI (**gastrointestinal**) problems. Again, poor hygiene compounded with the stress of long days of running makes these uncomfortable but unremarkable events. I always keep over the counter remedies like Imodium® in my first aid kit, and drink plenty of liquids to counteract fluid loss.

Blisters are seemingly a trivial problem and something that affects almost everyone – but neglect them at your peril. Blisters are sore; foot soreness can lead to running in funny, unnatural ways, which can in turn lead to muscle injury due to imbalance. Blisters also create open wound sites which give nasty germs – like *staphylococcus* – a direct path into your blood stream. It's critical to get them drained and properly disinfected. Let them dry at night and then just before running tape them to avoid further discomfort and friction. It's important to figure out why you got the damn thing in the first place, and then make appropriate changes. Bunched up socks? Badly fitting shoes? Rain-soaked socks? Lose the problem and avoid future blisters.

Apart from getting hit by a vehicle, the biggest life-threatening risk to the ultra stage runner is contracting a serious **antibiotic-resistant infection**. Immediate professional diagnosis and treatment is the only solution here. It appears that taking too many anti-inflammatories can hasten the spread of serious and even deadly infections like *necrotizing fasciitis*.

Shin splints are perhaps the most common injury complaint and can be very debilitating. "Shin splint" is a general term used to refer to a painful condition in the shins, which can eventually lead to stress fractures and even worse things like muscle necrosis. Shin splints are the evil twin of **Achilles tendonitis**. They are both very painful and slow to respond to treatment. Most runners, due to their natural gait and the terrain they're running on, will develop one or the other if they run far enough. You can always spot who is suffering from which on hills. The Achilles sufferers hobble on the way up; the shin splint folks hobble on the way down.

The problem of **sore feet** has been the consistent one that has affected me most during multiday races. I have tried many different shoe manufacturers, models, widths, sizes, footbeds and socks but, whatever I do, my feet still become very painful after a few long days on the road. It usually takes me a couple of months after a long race for the nerve damage in my feet to recede so that I can run comfortably again.

I've seen ultrarunners contend with a litany of other musculoskeletal issues due to the repetitive jarring and load bearing nature of running. **Joint problems** can affect knees, hips, and ankles. Bones in the foot, leg, or hip can develop mild to severe stress fractures. **Large muscle group injuries** – quads, hamstrings, calves, glutes and back – can also give major problems. And I've known at least two runners who've had to abandon due to **heart problems**, in the form of arrhythmia or abnormally high blood pressure. Scary stuff, and definitely a good signal to cease and desist immediately.

Injuries can often be worsened by what I'll call "compounding": an injury in one spot causes some kind of imbalance or favoring, which in turn causes secondary or even tertiary problems. When all this is served up with a plentiful helping of fatigue, ultra stage runners can face a world of hurt.

What can be done to treat these almost inevitable problems? Conventional wisdom recommends treatment which goes by the acronym **RICE** (Rest, Ice, Compression and Elevation):

– Resting is clearly impractical during a multiday race, so let's gloss over that as quickly as possible.
– Ice is traditionally very hard to come by in Europe, unlike the almost Titanic- sinking amounts served with every cold drink in the US. For the first time during Trans Europe 2009, Jan the medic thoughtfully brought along an ice making machine and would hand it out to those

in need. He was a very popular man amongst
the walking wounded each evening.
–   Compression socks are quite popular in Europe;
    several runners wore them every day of the race.
    I can't speak to their efficacy, but I personally
    don't like wearing tight things around my legs.
–   Many runners, including me, frequently
    elevated their legs while resting or sleeping.
    Even a few minutes before the start each day, a
    number of us would lie down on the gym floor
    hoping for some last-minute fluid drainage.

There are a number of other options which runners
use with varying degrees of success. Non-steroidal
anti-inflammatory drugs (**NSAIDs**) are used by
some in moderation, but these days are generally
looked down on by many ultra runners as a
dangerous way to go.   In large doses over time, they
compromise the digestive system, kidneys and liver.
I use them in small doses to counteract inflammation
in my feet and hip sometimes, but I've become much
more cautious and conservative with them than I
used to be.

Massage is a useful therapy, but I've always found it
hard to get appointments mid-race. **Taping** using
the voguish Kinesio® tape became very popular a
few years back, but folks seem to be reporting more
limited success with it these days. The many claims
on the Elastic Therapeutic Taping part of their
website seem rather ambitious to me.

One fascinating thing I have observed is what I'll
term "**dynamic healing.**" Conventional wisdom
says that injuries won't heal if you don't rest them.
Well, I have witnessed runners recover slowly from
terrible injuries as overuse has continued. It's as if

the body finally gives up complaining about being hurt and decides that it might as well just get on with it and start to heal.

And one last technique for dealing with injuries or illness is simple – good, old fashioned suffering. Remember:

"This ain't no party, this ain't no disco, this ain't no fooling around
No time for dancing, or lovey dovey, I ain't got time for that now"
- Talking Heads, "Life During Wartime"

SOME ULTRA APHORISMS

An aphorism is a "tersely phrased statement of a truth, opinion or principle." Here's a Top Ten list I've distilled from my ultrarunning career (running all day for many days gives you plenty of time to think about stuff like this):

1. **You can over-prepare and under-prepare, but over-preparing is worse.**

    Weekly distances on stage races are many times longer than any training week. Go into the race healthy, uninjured and well fed, and start slowly. I repeat – start slowly!

2. **Take care of injuries and illnesses as soon as they occur.**

    You will develop injuries which will make you miserable. And you will get sick. It is inevitable, but you will recover. Try to stay healthy and injury free, stay mentally positive, eat right and get rest – in that order.

3. **Expect every kind of weather and temperature, and you will not be disappointed.**

    If you spend long enough running down the road, you will encounter almost every form of climatic condition there is, short of hurricane, typhoon or tsunami. Do not assume that a calm, sunny morning will be followed by a picture perfect afternoon.

4. **You will not make it without comfortable footwear, hat, sunglasses, gloves and waterproof jacket.**

Dress in layers, and overdress at the start. Goretex® is your friend. Never leave home without directions, toilet paper, a little money, gloves, and some sugary snacks for low blood sugar emergencies.

5. **One step at a time, one kilometer at a time, one aid station at a time, one stage at a time, one week at a time, one country at a time.**

   Well, duh. Of course that's how you run a long race. But you have to "eat the elephant" in small bites, or you'll choke on the metaphor.

6. **Run your own race and don't obsess over details like pace and place.**

   Getting to the finish is the only thing that matters – just ask anyone who has DNF'd. Don't attempt to run up steep hills – it's a waste of valuable energy.

   The only person you're racing against is yourself – your "competitors" are really your allies.

7. **Quitting is harder than keeping going.**

   A DNF is a terrible thing, an incompletion, a failure. DNFs can hang over your head for years or even decades. Never, ever drop out unless there is a compelling medical issue, like a broken leg or a heart attack.

8. **Once underway, the only way to affect the outcome is attitude.**

   Sometimes you just have to tough it out. Two brief 'tude quotes I like:

   "Toughen up, Buttercup" – posted on my blog by co-worker Jeff Cross, when I was

suffering in Germany.
"Quit bitching!" - by Lance Armstrong, when Kevin Livingstone asked him about the effects of allergies in Austin.

9. **Don't underestimate or undervalue the help of others to get you to the finish.**
Great things happen when people work together, before and during the race. Race volunteers make all the difference. Their time is a priceless gift to you - so be gracious.

10. **Remember to be grateful for good luck.**
"Those who have succeeded at anything and don't mention luck are kidding themselves."
- Larry King

BIBLIOGRAPHY

Running the Trans America Footrace : Trials and Triumphs of Life on the Road
By Barry Lewis
Stackpole Books, 1994

A Step Beyond: A Definitive Guide to Ultrarunning
Edited by Don Allison
UltraRunning Publishers, 2004

Duel in the Sun
By John Brant
Rodale, 2006

Staying the Course : A Runner's Toughest Race
By Dick Beardsley and Maureen Anderson
University of Minnesota Press, 2002

Ultramarathon Man
By Dean Karnazes
Penguin Group, 2005

No Shortcuts to the Top
By Ed Viesturs with David Roberts
Broadway Books, 2006

The Engine 2 Diet
By Rip Esselstyn
Grand Central Publishing, 2008

What I Talk About When I Talk About Running
By Haruki Murakami
Random House, 2008

THANKS

My grateful thanks go to the following people, who helped me to become a transcontinental runner:

- To Ingo Schulze, Jean-Benoît Jaouen and Les Wright, who directed the wonderful races mentioned in this book, and to the outstanding teams of volunteers who supported them.

- To my friends from all over the world who ran these races with me, especially Christian Marti, Gérard Denis and Jean-Hervé Duchesne, all supported by their wonderful spouses.

- To Diana Wightman, Raife and Victoria Watson, Mike Wilen and Jan Straub, who kept me going through some very tough times on the road in Germany, France, Sweden and across Europe.

- To Leah Nyfeler, Valerie Pearcy and Jack Woodville London, for enthusiastically volunteering to help edit and improve this book, and to Tibor Ambrus and Helmut Dietz who took some of the photos.

- To the Austin running community, especially Carolyn, Ruth and Steve at Rogue Training Systems, and many hundreds of other coaches, runners and race organizers who make this such a great running city.

- To my friends and former co-workers at Hoover's Online in Texas and London.

- To Pam LeBlanc, Jim Swift, Bob Wischnia, and the good folks at Austin Monthly, for helping to publicize my adventures.

- To the board and members of Austin Runners Club and Hill Country Trail Runners, for showing an interest in my stories, and inspiring me to complete this book.

- To my wonderful family for putting up with me for so long – my parents, Bob and Nora, my speedy running kids Tracey, Rob and Tom, and the awesome athlete I'm very proud to call my wife, Claire.

- And lastly, thanks to two unrelated people with the same last name:

  ➤ To Barry Lewis for writing that wonderful book about Trans America 1992, which got me thinking about all this in the first place;

  ➤ And to the late Conrad Lewis, the martinet teacher who made me run around that god awful park in England so many times as a young boy.

I would not have made it without you all.

7501234R0

Made in the USA
Lexington, KY
28 November 2010